LEACOCK ON LIFE

LEACOCK
ON LIFE

EDITED BY GERALD LYNCH

UNIVERSITY OF TORONTO PRESS
Toronto Buffalo London

© University of Toronto Press Incorporated 2002
Toronto Buffalo London
Printed in Canada

ISBN 0-8020-3594-9

Printed on acid-free paper

National Library of Canada Cataloguing in Publication Data

Leacock, Stephen, 1869–1944
  Leacock on life

ISBN 0-8020-3594-9

I. Lynch, Gerald, 1953–   II. Title.

PS8523.E15A6 2002   C813'.52   C2002-901122-1
PR9199.3.L367A6 2002

University of Toronto Press acknowledges the financial assistance to its
publishing program of the Canada Council for the Arts and the Ontario
Arts Council.

University of Toronto Press acknowledges the financial support for its
publishing activities of the Government of Canada through the Book
Publishing Industry Development Program (BPIDP).

For my father,
Jim Lynch

The prudent husbandman, after having taken from his field all the straw that is there, rakes it over with a wooden rake and gets as much again. The wise child, after the lemonade jug is empty, takes the lemons from the bottom of it and squeezes them into a still larger brew. So does the sagacious author, after having sold his material to the magazines and been paid for it, clap it into book covers and give it another squeeze.

LEACOCK

All right. Life is just repetition.

LEACOCK

CONTENTS

REFERENCE KEY

AA   *Arcadian Adventures with the Idle Rich.* 1914. Rpt. Toronto: McClelland and Stewart–NCL, 1959.

AU   *Afternoons in Utopia: Tales of the New Time.* London: John Lane, 1932.

BB   *Behind the Beyond.* 1913. Rpt. Toronto: McClelland and Stewart–NCL, 1969.

BE   *The British Empire: Its Structure, Its Unity, Its Strength.* New York: Dodd, Mead, 1940.

BLB   *The Boy I Left behind Me.* Garden City, NY: Doubleday, 1946.

BP   *Back to Prosperity: The Great Opportunity of the Empire Conference.* London: Constable, 1932.

CD   *Charles Dickens: His Life and Work.* 1933. Rpt. Garden City, NY: Sun Dial Press, 1938.

CFF   *Canada: The Foundations of Its Future.* Montreal: Privately Printed, 1941.

CoD   *College Days.* London: John Lane, 1923.

DP   *The Dry Pickwick: And Other Incongruities.* London: John Lane, 1932.

DSP   'Democracy and Social Progress.' In *The New Era in Canada.* Ed. John O. Miller. Toronto: Dent, 1917. 13–33.

ELS   *Essays and Literary Studies.* Toronto: S.B. Gundy, 1916.

FF   *Further Foolishness: Sketches and Satires on the Follies of the Day.* 1916. Rpt. Toronto: McClelland and Stewart–NCL, 1968.

FrF   *Frenzied Fiction.* 1919. Rpt. Toronto: McClelland and Stewart–NCL, 1965.

GCA   'Greater Canada: An Appeal.' *University Magazine* 6 (April 1907): 132–41.

GF   *The Garden of Folly.* Toronto: S.B. Gundy, 1924.

HA   *The Hohenzollerns in America: With the Bolsheviks in Berlin, and Other Impossibilities.* Toronto: S.B. Gundy; New York: John Lane, 1919.

HH   *Humour and Humanity: An Introduction to the Study of Humour.* London: Thornton Butterworth, 1937.

HML   *Here Are My Lectures and Stories.* New York: Dodd, Mead, 1937.

HL   *Our Heritage of Liberty: Its Origin, Its Achievement, Its Crisis; a Book for War Time.* London: John Lane, 1942.

HoH   *Hellements of Hickonomics: In Hiccoughs of Verse Done in Our Social Planning Mill.* New York: Dodd, Mead, 1936.

HS   *Happy Stories Just to Laugh At.* New York: Dodd, Mead, 1943.

HTT   *Humour, Its Theory and Technique: With Examples and Samples; a Book of Discovery.* London: John Lane, 1935.

HTW   *How to Write.* New York: Dodd, Mead, 1943.

IM   *The Iron Man and the Tin Woman, and Other Futurities.* London: John Lane, 1929.

LaL   *Last Leaves.* 1945. Rpt. Toronto: McClelland and Stewart–NCL, 1970.

LL   *Literary Lapses.* 1910. Rpt. Toronto: McClelland and Stewart–NCL, 1957.

MDE   *My Discovery of England.* 1922. Rpt. Toronto: McClelland and Stewart–NCL, 1961.

MDW   *My Discovery of the West: A Discussion of East and West in Canada.* Boston and New York: Hale, Cushman and Flint, 1937.

MGC   'A Message to the Graduating Class of 1944.' *McGill News* 25 (Summer 1944): 7–8.

MLL   *Moonbeams from the Larger Lunacy.* 1915. Rpt. Toronto: McClelland and Stewart–NCL, 1964.
MT   *Mark Twain.* London: Peter Davies, 1932.
NN   *Nonsense Novels.* 1911. Rpt. Toronto: McClelland and Stewart–NCL, 1963.
OF   *Over the Footlights.* New York: Dodd, Mead, 1923.
OPM   *Other People's Money: An Outside View of Trusts and Investments.* Montreal: Royal Trust Co., 1947.
RU   *My Remarkable Uncle.* 1942. Rpt. Toronto: McClelland and Stewart–NCL, 1965.
SC   *Short Circuits.* 1928. Rpt. Toronto: McClelland and Stewart–NCL, 1967.
SS   *Sunshine Sketches of a Little Town.* 1912. Rpt. Ottawa: Tecumseh, 1996.
TMC   *Too Much College, or Education Eating Up Life: With Kindred Essays in Education and Humour.* New York: Dodd, Mead, 1939.
UR   *The Unsolved Riddle of Social Justice.* Toronto: S.B. Gundy, 1920.
WLS   'What Is Left of Adam Smith?' *Canadian Journal of Economics and Political Science* 1 (Feb. 1935): 41–51.
WW   *Winnowed Wisdom.* 1926. Rpt. Toronto: McClelland and Stewart–NCL, 1971.
WWD   *Wet Wit and Dry Humour.* New York: Dodd Mead, 1931.

INTRODUCTION

Stephen Leacock (1869–1944), the English-speaking world's best-known humorist from about 1910 till his death, Canadian cultural icon, needs no introduction. But of course Leacock dealt with this needs-no-introduction gambit, mock-petulantly showing disregard for the editorial need of shortcuts: '"Professor Stephen Leacock," said the chairman, every chairman, from Fort William to Victoria, – "needs no introduction." Owing to this bright thought, I never got any' (MDW 1). More brightly then, I begin again: Stephen Leacock had something to say about everything (even his own introduction), and all of it is still entertaining and relevant.

Leacock on Life begins properly with the preface to *Sunshine Sketches of a Little Town* (1912), where Leacock's authorial persona introduces himself to the world for the first time, giving the facts of his life in an ironic voice that is matched only by the *Skeches'* narrator on Mariposa. This is, I trust, a more telling observation than it may first appear, as it can help towards answering the much-vexed question of Leacock's true view of Mariposa, and consequently of the town on which Mariposa was based, Orillia, and of the country, Canada, which the town in the sunshine was imagined to represent. That is, despite the unrelenting irony and passing satiric shadows of *Sunshine Sketches*, Leacock may well have cherished Mariposa as he did his own life; and Leacock, apparently a stranger to self-doubt, thoroughly enjoyed his seventy-four years. But apart from its critical value as a clue to reading, the self-introduction that begins *Sunshine Sketches* remains the best entrée to the fascinating mind that is

Stephen Leacock writing. Every time I read this thumbnail autobiography, it impresses me as an unsurpassed masterpiece of droll self-presentation. Enjoy it attentively again: the perfectly modulated ironic tone throughout is as surprising as it ever was, every sentence is delightful, every word right.

With that to offer, I wouldn't dream of competing with Leacock writing on his own life, though it should prove helpful here to touch on some of the important incidents of that life.

Leacock was born in England and emigrated to Canada as a child of six, where the family precariously farmed near Lake Simcoe in central Ontario in conditions that could pass as pioneering. He was blessed with a devoted mother who, with financial help from her family back in England, saw to it that Stephen and his brothers and sisters were well educated at home and later (for the boys) at Upper Canada College; and though she had some money from her relatives, Agnes (née Butler) Leacock sacrificed a great deal to rear her children properly. After the University of Toronto and a Ph.D. in political economy from the University of Chicago in 1903, Leacock became a professor at McGill University, where he remained for more than three decades of success after success. For most of his adult life he divided his year between Montreal and the summer home in Orillia that has since become the Leacock Museum. Until his death from cancer of the throat (that pipe, those cigars), he was Canada's foremost man of letters, internationally renowned for his perennial books of humour and essays on everything from nickel mining to the fate of the Devil in modern times. Two of his books of humorous-satiric fiction, *Sunshine Sketches of a Little Town* (1912) and *Arcadian Adventures with the Idle Rich* (1914), will be read for as long as reading is enjoyed. Many a writer (such as Mordecai Richler repeatedly) has claimed that the hope of just one lasting book is what keeps a writer writing.

As a seventeen-year-old, Leacock drove his ineffectual father, Peter, to the train station and, brandishing a horsewhip, threatened to kill him if he ever returned. Peter didn't. Leacock idealized his remarkable uncle, E.P. Leacock (and immortalized him in the title piece of *My Remarkable Uncle*), though there is an unmistakable undertone of condescension in all his writings about that ostentatious man's life. Still, it's a safe guess that Leacock learned much about performative bluff and display from his father's younger brother, and likely found the first model for the *Sketches'* Josh Smith. He idolized Charles Dickens and Mark Twain, while acknowledging their faults as writers and men, and wrote critical biographies of both. Again, we can readily discern – read and hear – the influential confluence of the Englishman and the American in Leacock. He maintained a close relationship with his mother, relying on her counsel and sometimes heeding her literary advice, to the extent that, from its serial publication in the *Montreal Star* to book publication, he toned down passages of *Sunshine Sketches* that she thought too offensively close to home (and perhaps also because some of Leacock's Orillian neighbours 'jokingly' had threatened to sue him). He was driven to distraction by his wife's cancer, then deeply depressed by her death in 1925, and his books of the late 1920s, especially *Short Circuits* (1928), show a darkening of comic vision approaching the cynical. On the other hand, the revealingly titled *Winnowed Wisdom* of 1926 begins with the splendidly sustained 'The Outlines of Everything,' whose satire of a fast-paced and tasteless modernity is so good as to make me regret that Leacock didn't let the shadows in more often. But critics, and Canadians especially, are always asking Leacock to be something other than what he was – more satiric, a conventional novelist, more in line with fashionable thinking, etc. – when what he was is already so much.

If preponderantly enjoying his life, no less certain is it that Leacock had his share of disappointments. His son and only child, Stevie, was severely stunted in his physical growth, dying as a result, at least partially, of alcohol and prescription drug abuse. This is not to disregard Stephen Lushington Leacock's achievements in becoming a lecturer at McGill University and something of a writer in his own right (if nonetheless thanks to his worried father's influence). But I don't imagine it would have been an easy thing for even the most well-adjusted and gifted of children to live with Father Leacock. Supposedly, Leacock would play a parlour trick on visitors by having Stevie, who at twenty could pass for twelve, stand before an esteemed (and probably half-tanked) gathering and answer their sophisticated questions, so that Leacock could claim his boy was a prodigy. And in leaving this world, Stevie also left the doors and windows of the Orillia home thrown open to the elements and looters, causing irreparable damage to many of his father's remaining books and manuscripts.[1]

There are many reliable reports of those scorched by Stephen Leacock's hot temper (Leacock to a new servant boy: 'Bring me a small piece of ice, one about the size of your brain'; firing all the servants one day and hiring them back the next at increased wages).[2] But mainly he was a dutiful son, a good husband, an attentive father, a fair (and contrite) employer, a helpful teacher, and a loyal friend. And mostly his humour is humour: 'The kindly contemplation of the incongruities of life and the artistic expression thereof' (HH 15), as he originally defined it. For Leacock, the word 'kindly' recognizes the kinship of humanity as distinct from the divisive bent of satire; kindly humour aims for a laughing *with* as opposed to *at*.

Leacock was always engaged in politics, both in his writing and more actively. He stumped for the Conservative party in the 1911 general election, which they won on an exclusively anti-reciprocity (against freer trade with the US) platform, unseating Wilfrid Laurier's Liberals from the government benches. In the 1930s, Prime

---

1 See Albert and Theresa Moritz, *Leacock: A Biography* (Toronto: Stoddart, 1985), 325–6: 'Through 1956, Stevie continued to live at the lodge [of the Leacock home in Orillia], which had fallen into disrepair. He imitated his father's mannerisms, but in an erratic, painfully exaggerated fashion. He dressed sloppily and eccentrically, hired and fired servants and had himself driven everywhere in taxi cabs. Taking taxis became one of his hallmarks.'

2 A highly informative and entertaining source of reliable anecdotes of life with Leacock is Allan Anderson's *Remembering Leacock: An Oral History* (Ottawa: Deneau, 1983).

Minister R.B. Bennett himself urged Leacock to stand for Parliament, but he refused, as he'd refused others' invitations to do so both at home and in England. No less an authority than former student and senator Eugene Forsey believed that Leacock could have been anything he wanted to be, including prime minister of Canada. But for Leacock, practical politics appears to have been a spectator sport at which he served as interested commentator and sometimes ironic cheerleader. When he wrote wholeheartedly about politics, it was mostly to encourage citizens towards a greater idealism and communal consciousness. Whenever politics provides fodder for his humour, it is presented as nearly identical with business interests, or its increasing reliance on image and mass media is viewed both humorously and sceptically, and sometimes cynically. There is even some historical evidence to suggest that, on at least one occasion, Leacock himself was used by politicians and big business interests; specifically, that in his stumping for the Conservatives and protectionism in that 1911 campaign he was unwittingly the dupe of the Canadian Manufacturers' Association, who employed identity politics and exploited the British connection for less than patriotic ends. Or perhaps Leacock 'wittingly' allowed his considerable voice to be used. It must remain ever risky to second-guess the incomparably savvy Leacock on the business of Canadian politics. Consider: Why, in *Sunshine Sketches*' fictionalized version only a year after that most fractious of Canadian general elections, does he make the opportunistic, capitalistic, and hilariously changeable Josh Smith the anti-reciprocity Conservative candidate – that is, make the duplicitous Smith the figurehead of Leacock's own real party?

Leacock hated his ten years as a schoolteacher but loved his three decades as a university professor. Like many a highly accomplished professional, he had assumed that an exception would be made when it came time for his retirement at age sixty-five, even though he had helped draft McGill's mandatory retirement regulation. No exemption was forthcoming. Leacock vociferously resented his forced retirement for years. He probably came closest to making a fool of himself in railing against it, repeatedly referring to himself as part of some ousted 'senility gang.' There was also real biting humour in it, of course. When a *New York Times* reporter asked him what he thought of the university administrators who had forced him to retire, he said, 'I have plenty to say about the governors putting me out of the university ... but I have all eternity to say it in. I shall shout it down to them.'[3]

His last words to an attendant at Toronto General Hospital were: 'Did I behave pretty well? Was I a good boy?' I think his mother's ghost would have answered yes, as should we to the ghost of Leacock.

Leacock rose to international celebrity at a time when the printed word was beginning to have to compete with radio and the cinema for the public's attention; that is, when the frenetic modern age of the twentieth century came fully into its own, our wired world. In the 1920s, at the height of his fame, he was courted by the likes of Charlie Chaplin, and Douglas Fairbanks and Mary Pickford, to write screenplays. He refused (though he clearly had a talent for scenarios; his writings include a number of pieces in dramatic and screenplay format, for he was both intrigued by and suspicious of the movies, if viewing cinema's potential as exclusively for farce). In the 1930s he agreed to read from his work weekly on CBC radio in a twenty-six-week series that was cut before its completion. His performance was a failure, because his tactic of chuckling in anticipation of a joke, which by all accounts was infectious when experienced live, bombed on air. In the public lecture hall, Leacock was a masterful performer (which is probably why he insisted on having an audience of friends along for the radio show). But his gifts as a humorist are preeminently literary ones, and luckily for us the best performance is always playing on the page.

3 'Leacock Retired by McGill,' *New York Times*, 19 December 1935; qtd. in Ralph Curry, *Stephen Leacock: Humorist and Humanist* (Garden City, NY: Doubleday, 1959), 257.

From our perspective, Leacock can be seen as a late instance of that nearly extinct species, the popular essayist willing to write on any subject. In his time he shared the press's more plentiful pages with such of his essaying contemporaries as H.G. Wells, Hillaire Belloc, George Bernard Shaw, and G.K. Chesterton. Leacock and Chesterton met over a billiard game, which the two insisted on keeping private for its three-hour duration, and became friends.[4] In a piece poking fun at a fad for getting at the private person behind the public figure (an enduring fad – oxymoronic as that phrase is – become a contemporary obsession), Leacock concludes a pretty funny catalogue with the news that the corpulent Chesterton is, in private, actually quite thin. So good friends indeed, however distant the relationship, to level such a shot at the famously and self-consciously overweight Chesterton. The two men were of course distinctive writers and performers, but I would venture that their immediate rapport was based on a shared idealistic turn of mind, on an almost reluctant romanticism in the age of realism-naturalism, and on a refusal to suffer dangerous fools; perhaps too on the shared stress of being such distinguished public figures, forever in that increasingly darting public eye (thus the significance of the closed billiard game). But whatever the reasons for their friendship – and Leacock had a talent for lifelong friendship – the Chesterton connection offers an opportunity to quote from an essay on Chesterton by Wilfred Sheed. The first paragraph below describes the role of such popular essayists as Leacock, giving an idea of their literary milieu, that turn-of-the-twentieth-century cultural ethos; then in the second paragraph Sheed sarcastically indicates what we today are missing:

The turn of the century was a happy time for the light essay. Life was just serious enough, without being too serious. People of the reading persuasion had the time and patience to listen to abstract

4 For an account of this meeting, see Séamus O'Toole, 'MMB: The Galway Years,' in *Piggy: The Authoritative Text, Editorial Paraphernailia, Letters by Buchanan, Criticism*, ed. Ursula Hogg-Reave (Kiel, Germany: l&f verlag, 1996), 140–1.

discussion on every level of importance; and the popular essayist, the man who put things well, was expected to write with equal vivacity about chasing his hat, votes for women, and whither are we drifting. Naturally, he was expected to deal with each of these in the same well-known and beloved style.

After two wars, etc., much of this light-hearted discussion appears pretty thin and beside the point. Nowadays we like things to be either very funny or very serious, and that special blend of the two moods seems as a consequence curiously outdated. The humorist sticks firmly to his business (monotonously stamping his products 'joke,' 'joke,' 'joke'), and leaving the heavy stuff to the expert and the prophet. We are much quicker than our immediate fathers were to question an essayist's qualifications: and God help the contemporary light author who strays without the appropriate degrees into, say, economics, as Mr. Belloc did, or into history, *à la* Mr. Wells. Intelligence is no longer enough.[5]

Leacock, a professional economist and amateur (if widely published) historian, with degrees, comes at the tail-end of that more literary time. As much as he was Canada's Victorian-Edwardian (funny) man of letters, he was also something of a bridging figure to the essayists-comedians of the mid-to-late twentieth century. American (*New Yorker* magazine mostly) humorists such as Robert Benchley, Dorothy Parker, S.J. Perleman, Jack Benny and Woody Allen have acknowledged their debts to Leacock. In fact, Benchley idolized him, once providing the following blurb for a Leacock book: 'I have enjoyed Leacock's work so much that I have written everything he ever wrote – anywhere from one to five years after him ... P.S. In case the proof-reader thinks that I meant "I have read everything he ever wrote," please tell him I really meant "written".'[6]

---

5 Wilfred Sheed, 'On Chesterton,' in *G.K. Chesterton: A Half Century of Views*, ed. D.J. Conlon (Oxford and New York: Oxford UP, 1987), 162. I am grateful to David Rampton for bringing this essay to my attention.
6 See Curry, 358–9n20.

And I suspect that other readers will hear an anticipation of, say, the nonsensical Woody Allen style in this Leacockian fabrication of Darwin's diary: 'On the Antilles the common crow, or decapod, has two feet while in the Galapagos Islands it has a third. This third foot, however, does not appear to be used for locomotion, but merely for conversation' (WW 9). Leacock can thus be seen to serve as the most significant figure of continuity between nineteenth-century comic writing and that of the twentieth century from its beginning to end, especially in North America but in England and elsewhere as well.

So, though the wider reading public of the early twenty-first century may no longer be treated (both entertained and 'physicked,' as by one of Carlyle's cultural physicians of the age) by men and women of letters, Leacock the humorist does have his influential successors among the most popular American humorists. And in Canada he is succeeded by such writers as Robertson Davies, Eric Nicol, Mordecai Richler, Erika Ritter, and Charles Gordon, while other such eminent Canadian writers as F.R. Scott and Hugh Hood also acknowledged their fellow Montrealer's lasting influence on their work. Even the most ardent Canadian cultural nationalists can't help but betray a colonial impressionability at the places Leacock turns up – praised by Samuel Beckett, mentioned by Jorge Luis Borges as the only Canadian writer he knows, and so forth.

I have often suspected that Richler learned one of his recurrent stylistic turns from Leacock: the flat statement big with irony. You see this rhetorical feature in Leacock in the capping of such passages as that on the up-to-date Episcopal church that boasts a 'Men's Guild, with a bowling-alley and a swimming-bath deep enough to drown two young men at a time, and a billiard-room with seven tables. It is the rector's boast that with a Guild House such as that there is no need for any young man of the congregation to frequent a saloon. Nor is there' (AA 101). Richler brought this technique – call it minimalist capping – to its apogee, often speaking volumes in one word set off as its own paragraph. It's worth noting that one of the last things Richler wrote was an introduction to a new edition of *Sunshine Sketches* in 2000, wherein he credits that book with being 'the first work to establish a Canadian voice,' an observation which weightily bears comparison with Hemingway's landmark claim that all modern American fiction flows from *Huckleberry Finn*[7] (and I noticed, too, in one video clip of the fusillade of media attention following his death last year that Richler invoked Leacock's bounding Lord Ronald to characterize Canada's directionally challenged Parliament).

On the other side of the temporal continuum, Leacock himself learned from such predecessors as Jonathan Swift, Henry Fielding, and Mark Twain the comic rewards of the mock-epic and mock-heroic, mainstays of his style. He also learned from them (especially Swift) the comic impact of making the metaphoric literal, as is evidenced by Miss Cleghorn's longing look at the picnic setting of the Mariposa Belle excursion: 'The scene is all so quiet and still and unbroken, that Miss Cleghorn, – the sallow girl in the telephone exchange, that I spoke of – said she'd like to be buried there. But all the people were so busy getting their baskets and gathering up their things that no one had time to attend to it' (SS 45). Funny, even when its effect has been given away by me.

To be fair, Leacock was both beneficiary and exploited subject of the growing mass communication-consumerist culture that paid him well for the wealth of humour he delivered too frequently, and often too much to formula. It's true, as many complain, that some of Leacock's humour is strained; true, because too much of it reads as though forced in, if not the hothouse, then the boathouse at Old Brewery Bay on Lake Couchiching, where he did much of his writing before the household was up (he claimed that the name Old Brewery Bay – christening by Leacock – had been known to make people thirsty by correspondence as far away as Nevada). A concen-

---

7 Mordecai Richler, introduction to *Sunshine Sketches of a Little Town*, by Stephen Leacock (London: Prion, 2000), xiii. Hemingway's remark can be found in *The Green Hills of Africa* (New York: Charles Scribner's, 1935), 19.

trated period of reading as much Leacock as can be got is not the best way to appreciate him. Always there is the very clever idea, cleverly expressed, but sometimes then tediously worked out. When Leacock nods it's no mere dip of the chin, but a drop as if he would split his writing table with a karate-chopping forehead – an unforgivable fall into the forced extended joke, as tiresome to read as (I imagine) it must have been to write. But that original idea and its first expression can be brilliant, an inspiration of humorous-satiric thought. Consequently, such a book as *Leacock on Life* actually has the advantage of presenting the best of Leacock at his best and the best of his worst as well. As he himself said, aware no doubt that he was churning it out at times, a writer should be judged on his best.

When I began reading for this book, I had thought there would be more epigrams and witty one-liners than proved to be the case. The one-liners are there (it was easy to recall twenty or so pointed sayings for a proposal to the publisher) and they are here, but it soon became clear that Leacock is not at his best as a composer of epigrams. He is rather, as he always claimed to be, a humorist. His style and effectiveness require a few sentences, sometimes a short paragraph, at other times a couple of paragraphs. This is not just for the sake of conveying an adequate sense of the subject but also for the writing's distinctive rhythms and the perfect pacing of the humorous observation to climax. With humour especially, prose rhythm and pacing are essential to full appreciation – in themselves as literary art, and in order to hear the famous Leacock voice speaking in a prose that he seems to have played out as easily as fishing line, and as expertly hooked the reader. There should be no doubt, though, that Leacock laboured at his vocation, crafted that Leacock voice, worked the writing in service to a Victorian ethic that might have made Carlyle himself smile. So there is need for a little room to let Leacock's observations breathe. Let us not always be demanding the sort of rapid-fire stand-up routine that Sheed laments as our lot, the Gatling-gun comic assault that tires more quickly than Leacock ever does or will.

For that matter, let us let Leacock not always have to be funny, *on*, or as he means it, *it*. As he wrote of Izaak Walton, author of the seventeenth-century fisherman's classic, *The Compleat Angler*, let us take time to see 'what Stephen Leacock can teach us.' As an example of what I mean along these lines, I include such as the longish passage from *Sunshine Sketches* describing the ostensibly laughable scene of Peter Pupkin's first sighting of his life's love, Zena Pepperleigh (Leacock's names are just about always perfectly representative, clearly another influence of Dickens, who would have learned it from Fielding and Smollett). Such a passage shows to fine effect Leacock's skill at tuning the Leacock voice in a typical movement from ironic detachment, to sentimental interest, to wholehearted endorsement – here, of the ideal of romantic love generally, and specifically of the experience of being young and in love in the sunshine of Mariposa (in fact, it's the loving vision of Pupkin and his author which creates the sunshine view of Mariposa and *Sunshine Sketches*, and makes kindly humour possible). Other such passages at shorter length, such as Leacock's account of his visit to Versailles, show him adept at manipulating that voice and attitude to indicate complex human psychology: in the Versailles piece, the essential futility of consumer tourism, even of doomed desire itself, and the Leacock persona's refusal to submit. Better to indulge in a cigar and a glass of wine at a nearby café – consuming humanely to counter a crasser consumption – to browse a brochure describing the palace ... pastimes which are then followed by the characteristically nonsensical promise to visit Versailles should he ever get the opportunity. *Leacock on Life* includes only one whole essay, ending with his reflections on growing old. If there's a better humorous take on aging and death, I'd like to be told of it before passing on to my just punishment.

The title *Leacock on Life* suits a Leacock compilation for other than the obvious descriptive reason. His books reveal an over-fondness for alliterative titles: *Literary Lapses, Sunshine Sketches, Arcadian*

Adventures, Nonsense Novels, Behind the Beyond, Further Foolishness, Frenzied Fiction, and so on.

What were my criteria of selection?

Did I censor Leacock?

A few times, to answer the second question first. Leacock, a life-long believer in the supremacy of peoples of British stock, could be racist, and globally so (which actually dulls the point of it, for me anyway, his not being overly particular or personal in his prejudices). Sometimes a racial slur gets mixed up in a good bit of writing, and these passages I left out without sacrificing much but offended feelings. Although such of Leacock's remarks are offensive, there is never anything ugly or hateful in them. They represent (and could do so usefully for cultural-historical study if we weren't so conditioned in our response to them) attitudes that were as much in the air of Leacock's time as in our own are, say, our continuing tolerance of eating our fellow creatures and managing to live well in proximity to dehumanizing poverty (both of which I do comfortably). Who can predict how the future will judge us, especially the well-off, food-and-fuel-guzzling portion of us in this narrowest wedge of the pie where all the fruit has been packed? We can only hope that our descendants will be *kinder* to us on such matters than we mostly are to our ancestors. But there was really no call to include in such a book as the present one Leacock's few racist remarks. Luckily, Leacock was an unapologetic self-plagiarist (see the first epigraph to the present volume), and what was expressed offensively in one place could be found improved in another. Regardless, perhaps all too insensitively, in the 'Other Nations' section of this book I've retained all the nasty things he had to say about such as the Irish (*c'est moi*), the Scotch (they can take it), and such other fair game as the British, French, Germans, Americans, and Canadians.

As for the first question above regarding my criteria of selection: I chose whatever I most liked, if with a determination to entertain readers and to represent Leacock's wide range of interests.

To our credit, Leacock remains a perennial best-seller in Canada.

Malcolm Ross, founder of McClelland and Stewart's New Canadian Library series in the late 1950s, the library of affordable paperback reprints that first made the teaching of Canadian literature widely possible, said that at first he regularly inserted a Leacock book just to carry the fledgling NCL series. The author of some eighty books and pamphlets and of countless essays, Leacock was as witty and wise as he was prolific and popular, and as sharp as he was humane. Possessed of the rarest of gifts for humorous observation ('the incongruities of life') and memorable phrasing ('the artistic expression thereof'), his views provide a uniquely Canadian take on life, a version which continues to appeal as well to the rest of the English-speaking world (and widely in translation). Perhaps needless to say, *Leacock on Life* should be sampled regularly rather than read straight through. The hope is that it will lead new readers to Leacock whole, and remind his old friends why they should revisit him at length.

But here's the lasting attraction Leacock holds for me, the real value that my latest reading of his body of work has brought home again: he possessed an ever-energized, built-in 'bullshit detector,' that first requisite of a satirist-humorist if not, as Hemingway contended in coining the phrase, of a writer generally (because so many aspiringly serious writers are too full of the substance to be detected). For this reason alone Leacock should continue to be invaluable to us all, Canadians and the less fortunate equally. He is a safeguard against the hypocrisy of others and ourselves; or, if that sounds too harsh for Leacock, he is a reminder of our tendency individually and en masse towards damn foolishness (he kept a file folder labelled 'Letters from damn fools'). And he is a constant reminder of what we can be, individually, as a community, as Canadians, as human beings. And as funny as that communicative three-legged bird he created for Darwin.

LEACOCK ON LIFE

HIS LIFE

I know no way in which a writer may more fittingly introduce his work to the public than by giving a brief account of who and what he is. By this means some of the blame for what he has done is very properly shifted to the extenuating circumstances of his life.

I was born at Swanmoor, Hants, England, on December 30, 1869. I am not aware that there was any particular conjunction of the planets at the time, but should think it extremely likely. My parents migrated to Canada in 1876, and I decided to go with them. My father took up a farm near Lake Simcoe, Ontario. This was during the hard times of Canadian farming, and my father was just able by great diligence to pay the hired men and, in years of plenty, to raise enough grain to have seed for the next year's crop without buying any. By this process my brothers and I were inevitably driven off the land, and have become professors, business men, and engineers, instead of being able to grow up as farm labourers. Yet I saw enough of farming to speak exuberantly in political addresses of the joy of early rising and the deep sleep both of body and intellect that is induced by honest manual toil.

I was educated at Upper Canada College, Toronto, of which I was head boy in 1887. From there I went to the University of Toronto, where I graduated in 1891. At the University I spent my entire time in the acquisition of languages, living, dead, and half-dead, and knew nothing of the outside world. In this diligent pursuit of words I spent about sixteen hours of each day. Very soon after graduation I had forgotten the languages, and found myself intellectually bankrupt. In other words I was what is called a distinguished graduate, and, as such, I took to school teaching as the only trade I could find that needed neither experience nor intellect. I spent my time from 1891 to 1899 on the staff of Upper Canada College, an experience which has left me with a profound sympathy for the many gifted and brilliant men who are compelled to spend their lives in the most dreary, the most thankless, and the worst paid profession in the world. I have noted that of my pupils, those who seemed the laziest and the least enamoured of books are now rising to eminence at the bar, in business, and in public life; the really promising boys who took all the prizes are now able with difficulty to earn the wages of a clerk in a summer hotel or a deck hand on a canal boat.

In 1899 I gave up school teaching in disgust, borrowing enough money to live upon for a few months, and went to the University of Chicago to study economics and political science. I was soon appointed to a Fellowship in political economy, and by means of this and some temporary employment by McGill University, I survived until I took the degree of Doctor of Philosophy in 1903. The meaning of this degree is that the recipient of instruction is examined for the last time in his life, and is pronounced completely full. After this, no new ideas can be imparted to him.

From this time, and since my marriage, which had occurred at this period, I have belonged to the staff of McGill University, first as lecturer in Political Science, and later as head of the department of Economics and Political Science. As this position is one of the prizes of my profession, I am able to regard myself as singularly fortunate. The emolument is so high as to place me distinctly above the policemen, postmen, street-car conductors, and other salaried officials of the neighbourhood, while I am able to mix with the poorer of the business men of the city on terms of something like equality. In point of leisure, I enjoy more in the four corners of a single year than a business man knows in his whole life. I thus have what the business man can never enjoy, an ability to think, and, what is still better, to stop thinking altogether for months at a time.

I have written a number of things in connection with my college life – a book on Political Science, and many essays, magazine articles, and so on. I belong to the Political Science Association of America, to the Royal Colonial Institute, and to the Church of England. These things, surely, are a proof of respectability. I have had some small connection with politics and public life. A few years ago I went all round the British Empire delivering addresses on Imperial organization. When I state that these lectures were followed almost immediately by the Union of South Africa, the Banana Riots in Trinidad, and the Turco-Italian war, I think the reader can form some idea of their importance. In Canada I belong to the Conservative party, but as yet I have failed entirely in Canadian politics, never having received a contract to build a bridge, or make a wharf, nor to construct even the smallest section of the Transcontinental Railway. This, however, is a form of national ingratitude to which one becomes accustomed in this Dominion.

Apart from my college work, I have written two books, one called 'Literary Lapses' and the other 'Nonsense Novels.' Each of these is published by John Lane (London and New York), and either of them can be obtained, absurd though it sounds, for the mere sum of three shillings and sixpence. Any reader of this preface, for example, ridiculous though it appears, could walk into a bookstore and buy both of these books for seven shillings. Yet these works are of so humorous a character that for many years it was found impossible to print them. The compositors fell back from their task suffocated with laughter and gasping for air. Nothing but the intervention of the linotype machine – or rather, of the kind of men who operate it – made it possible to print these books. Even now people have to be very careful in circulating them, and the books should never be put into the hands of persons not in robust health.

Many of my friends are under the impression that I write these humorous nothings in idle moments when the wearied brain is unable to perform the serious labours of the economist. My own experience is exactly the other way. The writing of solid, instructive stuff fortified by facts and figures is easy enough. There is no trouble in writing a scientific treatise on the folk-lore of Central China, or a statistical enquiry into the declining population of Prince Edward Island. But to write something out of one's own mind, worth reading for its own sake, is an arduous contrivance only to be achieved in fortunate moments, few and far between. Personally, I would sooner have written 'Alice in Wonderland' than the whole Encyclopaedia Britannica. (SS xv–xvii)

I was born in Victorian England, on December thirtieth in 1869, which is exactly the middle year of Queen Victoria's reign. ... I am certain that I have never got over it. (BLB 9)

When I was a boy of six, my father brought us, a family flock, to settle on an Ontario farm. We lived in an isolation unknown, in these days of radio, anywhere in the world. We were thirty-five miles from a railway. There were no newspapers. Nobody came and went. There was nowhere to come and go. In the solitude of the dark winter nights the stillness was that of eternity. (RU 14)

To me as a child the farm part seemed just one big stink. It does still: the phew! of the stable – not so bad as the rest; the unspeakable cowshed, sunk in the dark below a barn, beyond all question of light or ventilation, like a mediæval oubliette; the henhouse, never cleaned and looking like a guano-deposit island off the coast of Chile, in which the hens lived if they could and froze dead if they couldn't; the pigsties, on the simple Upper Canada fashion of a log pen and a shelter behind, about three feet high. Guano had nothing on them. (BLB 59)

And all this time, although we didn't know, for my mother kept it hidden from us, at intervals my father drank, drove away to the village in the evening to return late at night after we were in bed, or lay round the farm too tired to work, and we thought it was the sun. And the more he drank, the more the farm slid sideways and downhill, and the more the cloud of debt, of unpaid bills, shadowed it over, and the deeper the shadow fell, the more he drank. My mother, I say, hid it all from us for years with a devotion that never faltered. My father, as he drank more, changed towards us from a superman and hero to a tyrant, from easy and kind to fits of brutality. I was small enough to escape from doing much of the farm chores and farm work. But I carry still the recollection of it – more, no doubt, than Jim or Dick ever did. In fact, the sight and memory of what domestic tyranny in an isolated, lonely home, beyond human help, can mean helped to set me all the more firmly in the doctrine of the rights of man and Jefferson's liberty. (BLB 95)

Meantime, as my father had vanished into space, my mother was still on the old farm with eight children younger than I to look after and with an income of, I think, eighty dollars a month to do it on. Of my two elder brothers, Jim was in Winnipeg with some small job in the courthouse, but quite unable to send money home, and Dick in the Northwest Mounted Police had nothing to spare from his pay. How my mother managed in the ensuing years before any of us could help her I do not know. I imagine the answer is that she drifted into debt and stayed there. Even when we could presently give her money it was merely applied over the surface of the debt below like a warm growth of Arctic flowers in the sun over cold frozen muskeg. (BLB 154–5)

When I was a student at the University of Toronto thirty years ago [ca. 1922], I lived – from start to finish – in seventeen different boarding houses. As far as I am aware these houses have not, or not yet, been marked with tablets. But they are still to be found in the vicinity of McCaul and Darcy and St. Patrick Streets. Anyone who doubts the truth of what I have to say may go and look at them.

I was not alone in the nomadic life that I led. There were hundreds of us drifting about in this fashion from one melancholy habitation to another. We lived as a rule two or three in a house, sometimes alone. We dined in the basement. We always had beef, done up in some way after it was dead, and there were always soda biscuits on the table. They used to have a brand of soda biscuits in those days in the Toronto boarding houses that I have not seen since. They were better than dog biscuits but with not so much snap. My contemporaries will all remember them. A great many of the leading barristers and professional men of Toronto were fed on them. (MDE 93)

I spent ten and a half years of my life (February 1889–July 1899) in teaching school, and I liked the last day of it as little as I liked the first. (BLB 151)

Fifty years ago I was a resident master in a boarding-school, a sort of all-day-and-all-night job, with a blind wall in front of it. To find a way out of it, and on, I took to getting up at five o'clock in the morning and studying political economy for three hours, every day, before school breakfast. This process so sharpened my sense of humour that I earned enough money by it to go away and study political economy; and that, you see, kept up my sense of humour like those self-feeding machines. (RU 50)

As I have the good luck to be a graduate of four different Canadian Universities, I am able to be all things to all men. (MDW 268)

The author of this book offers it to the public without apology. The reviewers of his previous work of this character have presumed, on inductive grounds, that he must be a young man from the most westerly part of the Western States, to whom many things might be pardoned as due to the exuberant animal spirits of youth. They were good enough to express the thought that when the author grew up and became educated there might be hope for his intellect. This expectation is of no avail. All that education could do in this case has been tried and has failed. (NN unpaginated preface)

To avoid all error as to the point of view, let me say in commencing that I am a Liberal Conservative, or, if you will, a Conservative Liberal with a strong dash of sympathy with the Socialist idea, a friend of Labour, and a believer in Progressive Radicalism. I do not desire office but would take a seat in the Canadian Senate at five minutes notice. (HA 232)

It is peculiar about The Woman [in popular fiction ca. 1916] that she never seems to wear a dress – always a 'gown.' Why this is, I cannot tell. In the good old stories that I used to read, when I could still read for the pleasure of it, the heroines – that was what they used to be called – always wore dresses. But now there is no heroine, only a woman in a gown. I wear a gown myself – at night. It is made of flannel and reaches to my feet, and when I take my candle and go out to the balcony where I sleep, the effect of it on the whole is not bad. But as to its 'revealing every line of my figure' – as The Woman's gown is always said to – and as to its 'suggesting even more than it reveals' – well, it simply does *not*. So when I talk of 'gowns' I speak of something that I know all about. (FF 25)

Let no one think, from what was said above, of the silence and peace of the North that I am trying to depict it as a vast frozen emptiness. Far be it from me to fall into that worn-out fallacy of the lifelessness of the North. If I ever shared it, I was cured of it long ago by an angry letter I once received from Vilhjalmar Stefansson, an angry letter that proved the beginning of a personal friendship of over twenty years. I had written a little book called *The Adventures of the Far North*, and had spoken in it of the North as if 'Here in this vast territory civilization has no part and life no place. Life struggles northward only to die out in the Arctic cold.'

Stefansson, who takes a personal pride in the North and regards Baffin Bay as a superior social centre to Naragansett Beach, felt affronted and wrote, in substance: 'You may be a h— of a humorist, but what you don't know about the North would fill a book. Don't you understand that the North is full of flowers and butterflies and life everywhere?' I answered back mildly: 'I meant further north still. The thing must stop somewhere.' But I learned the lesson, and I know now that it is just a poet's fancy to speak of the Great North as 'silent and untenanted.' (MDW 249–50)

Ernest Shackleton I knew also, and well. It is not generally known, for it has never been made history, that after the war Shackleton planned a Canadian polar expedition to explore the Beaufort Sea. He had wanted to go south again, but the British admiralty were very half-hearted about giving him support. So he turned to Canada and came to Montreal to raise money. I was one of those who tried to help in this, and, with the government's and private generosity, we soon had plenty of money in sight for the expedition. Exploration is as cheap as human life itself. I arranged on behalf of Shackleton for the services of a corps of young McGill scientists. Then he asked me if I would like to go as historiographer, and I said yes. I knew McGill would spare me. Any college would send its staff to the Beaufort Sea any time. I said I needed no pay, and so for twenty-four hours I was historiographer of the Beaufort Sea Canadian Expedition.

But it came to a sudden end. I said to Shackleton that I would supply all my own Scotch whiskey for the year's trip, as I didn't want to be a charge on the ship. And he said they didn't take whiskey on polar expeditions and, outside of the medicine chest, didn't allow it. Another illusion of the North shattered! I always thought that explorers, the ship once well set in the ice and buried in snow, went down below with a pack of cards and a keg of whiskey. But it seems not. They take observations. I resigned, and a little later news came that the admiralty had gone right about face and Shackleton was given a ship, and he went south and never came back. (MDW 252-3)

∽

Old indeed they [former classmates] looked: especially at first sight, old and furrowed and not hair enough on half a dozen of them for one rugby-football player of the '90's. But as you looked at them their faces changed back to shape again, the lines faded out, and with a drink or two, even their hair came back.

Old of course: for my own sixty-seventy birthday fell in when I was at Victoria on December 30, 1936.

It is amazing how the years slip away. I had got old and hadn't noticed it. And, of course, there is always the regret for the wasted time, the things that one might have done.

Look at the Emperor Charles the Fifth of Spain; long before he was my age he had ruled over half Europe and retired into a monastery to pray, and I haven't even started; and George III! At my age he'd been crazy twice, and had got over it. I haven't.

Someone in Vancouver said to me that it made him feel old to think that so many of his friends are dead. I told him I had got past that. I am old enough to expect them to be dead and they keep getting resurrected. My trouble is resurrection. They suddenly appear in clubs and hotels and say, 'Don't you know me?' and I answer, 'Go away; dematerialize yourself; don't haunt me.'

I am sure that lots of other men of my age suffer from these cases of premature resurrection. Some of them peculiarly distressing. I recall the incident of my old friend Boygate of Montreal. I am sure he won't mind, I mean wouldn't have minded, my mentioning his name thus in print. I came into my Club one afternoon (the University Club, next door to McGill University, Quebec License), and it suddenly occurred to me how greatly I missed Boygate now that he was gone: I wished that while he was still with us, I had seen more of him, had taken more occasion to sit with him round the Club, of which he, like myself, was a charter member. I realized that I had always been too self-centred, too much in a hurry to break away, had all too little appreciated the company of my friends. Ah, well, too late to change now! And just while I was feeling these regrets, in he walked! 'Boygate!' I exclaimed, shaking hands warmly while my eyes almost filled with tears. To think of it! Here he was alive again, either resurrected or never dead, it didn't matter which. 'Hullo! hullo!' he said warmly in return, 'come on up to the lounge and let's sit and have a talk.' 'Boygate,' I said, looking at my watch, as the world of customary habit closed round me, 'I'm sorry! I have to rush off to a meeting, – another time, eh?'

So what was the use of his resurrection after all. Life is like that. It's well they don't come back. (MDW 262–4)

AMERICA

But we infer even from our hurried view of the outskirts of the capital that if any bull wants silk hosiery that neither rips nor tears, he is exactly in the right place for it; and that Washington is exactly in the centre of the yeast district, the canned soup area, that all the great modern medical inventions such as HUMPO, JUMPO, and ANTIWHEEZE are sold there, and that we can get all the soap we want; – in short, look about us – here are Rooms with Beds at $1.50! Meals à la carte, Suspenders, Garters, Ice Cream in the Block, Radios, Gramophones, Elixirs of Life, Funeral Directors Open all Night, Real Estate, Bungalows, Breakfast Foods –

In truth – this is America indeed. (SC 23)

'I am an old man now, gentlemen,' Bagshaw said, 'and the time must soon come when I must not only leave politics, but must take my way towards that goal from which no traveller returns.'

There was a deep hush when Bagshaw said this. It was understood to imply that he thought of going to the United States. (SS 132)

FRIDAY [1916, President Woodrow Wilson's diary]. Rose early and tried to sweep out the White House. Had little heart for it. The dust gathers in the corners. How did Roosevelt manage to keep it so clean? An idea! I must get a vacuum cleaner! But where can I get a vacuum? Took my head in my hands and thought: problem solved. (FF 147)

⸙

The Americans are a queer people: they don't give a damn. All the world criticizes them and they don't give a damn. All the world writes squibs like this about them and they don't give a damn. Foreigner visitors come and write them up: they don't give a damn. Lecturers lecture at them: they don't care. They are told they have no art, no literature, and no soul. They never budge. Moralists cry over them, criminologists dissect them, writers shoot epigrams at them, prophets foretell the end of them, and they never move. Seventeen brilliant books analyse them every month: they don't read them. The Europeans threaten to unite against them: they don't mind. Equatorial Africa is dead sour on them: they don't even know it. The Chinese look on them as full of Oriental cunning: the English accuse them of British stupidity: the Scotch call them close-fisted: the Italians say they are liars: the French think their morals loose, and the Bolsheviks accuse them of communism.

But that's all right. The Americans don't give a damn: don't need to: never did need to. That is their salvation. (DP 92–3)

AUDIENCES

Most people tire of a lecture in ten minutes; clever people can do it in five. Sensible people never go to lectures at all. (MDE 148–9)

Appreciation grows the more it is divided. (HTW 20)

The city in which I live is overrun with little societies, clubs and associations, always wanting to be addressed. So at least it is in appearance. In reality the societies are composed of presidents, secretaries and officials, who want the conspicuousness of office, and a large list of other members who won't come to the meetings. (MDE 150–1)

'Gentlemen – if you are such, which I doubt. I realize that the paper which I have read on "Was Hegel a deist?" has been an error. I spent all winter on it and now I realize that not one of you pups knows who Hegel was or what a deist is. Never mind. It is over now, and I am glad. But just let me say this, only this, which won't keep you a minute. Your chairman has been good enough to say that if I come again you will get together a capacity audience to hear me. Let me tell you that if your society waits for its next meeting till I come to address you again, you will wait indeed. In fact, gentlemen – I say it very frankly – it will be in another world.' (MDE 152–3)

❧

And, as for audiences, for intelligence, for attention – well, if I want to find listeners who can hear and understand about the great spaces of Lake Huron, let me tell of it, every time face to face with the blue eyes of the Infant Class, fresh from the infinity of spaces greater still. Talk of grown-up people all you like, but for listeners let me have the Infant Class with their pinafores and their Teddy Bears and their feet not even touching the floor, and Mr. Uttermost may preach to his heart's content of the newer forms of doubt revealed by the higher criticism. (SS 82)

❧

When I was lecturing at Victoria, B.C., I went into the hotel barber shop to get my hair cut. The barber passed his comb back and forward through my hair and said:

'Well, sir, if I had a head of hair like yours, I'd make an awful lot of money selling hair tonic.'

'Yes,' I answered, 'and if I was as bald as you are, I could double my fees as a humorist.'

We parted with expressions of mutual esteem.

I told the story that night to my audience. But he's still telling it to his. (HML 29)

❧

This is the real public. It is not, of course, ignorant in the balder sense. A large part of it is technically, highly educated and absorbs the great mass of the fifty thousand college degrees granted in America each year [ca. 1916]. But it has an instinctive horror of 'learning,' such as a cat feels towards running water. It has invented for itself the ominous word 'highbrow' as a sign of warning placed over things to be avoided. This word to the American mind conveys much the same 'taboo' as haunts the tomb of a Polynesian warrior, or the sacred horror that enveloped in ancient days the dark pine grove of a Sylvan deity. (ELS 235)

The reading public is as wayward and as fickle as a bee among the flowers. It will not long pause anywhere, and it easily leaves each blossom for a better. But like the bee, while impelled by an instinct that makes it search for sugar, it sucks in therewith its solid sustenance.

I am not quite certain that the bee does exactly do this; but it is just the kind of thing that the bee is likely to do. And in any case it is precisely the thing which the reading public does. (UR 103)

The lights flick up. There is a great burst of applause. The curtain rises and falls. Lady Cicely and Mr. Harding and Sir John all come out and bow charmingly. There is no trace of worry on their faces, and they hold one another's hands. Then the curtain falls and the orchestra breaks out into a winter-garden waltz. The boxes buzz with discussion. Some of the people think that Lady Cicely is right in claiming the right to realise herself; others think that before realising herself she should have developed herself; others ask indignantly how she could know herself if her husband refused to let her be herself. But everybody feels that the subject is a delicious one.

Those of the people who have seen the play before very kindly explain how it ends, so as to help the rest to enjoy it. (BB 24)

As far as I know that chairman never knew his error [with Leacock's name]. At the close of my lecture he said that he was sure that the audience 'were deeply indebted to Mr. Learoyd,' and then with a few words of rapid, genial apology buzzed off, like a humming bird, to other avocations. But I have amply forgiven him: anything for kindness and geniality; it makes the whole of life smooth. If that chairman ever comes to my home town he is hereby invited to lunch or dine with me, as Mr. Learoyd or under any name that he selects. (MDE 163)

Witness this (word for word) introduction that was used against me by a clerical chairman in a quiet spot in the south of England:

'Not so long ago, ladies and gentlemen,' said the vicar, 'we used to send out to Canada various classes of our community to help build up that country. We sent out our labourers, we sent out our scholars and professors. Indeed we even sent out our criminals. And now,' with a wave of his hand towards me, 'they are coming back.'

There was no laughter. An English audience is nothing if not literal; and they are as polite as they are literal. They understood that I was a reformed criminal and as such they gave me a hearty burst of applause. (MDE 165–6)

To one experience of my tour as a lecturer I shall always be able to look back with satisfaction. I nearly had the pleasure of killing a man with laughing: and this in the most literal sense. American lecturers often dreamed of doing this. I nearly did it. The man in question was a comfortable apoplectic-looking man with the kind of merry rubicund face that is seen in countries where they don't have prohibition. He was seated near the back of the hall and was laughing uproariously. All of a sudden I realized that something was happening. The man had collapsed sideways on to the floor; a little group of men gathered about him; they lifted him up and I could see them carrying him out, a silent and inert mass. As in duty bound I went right on with my lecture. But my heart beat high with satisfaction. I was sure that I had killed him. The reader may judge how high these hopes rose when a moment or two later a note was handed to the chairman who then asked me to pause for a moment in my lecture and stood up and asked, 'Is there a doctor in the audience?' A doctor rose and silently went out. The lecture continued; but there was no more laughter; my aim had now become to kill another of them and they knew it. They were aware that if they started laughing they might die. In a few minutes a second note was handed to the chairman. He announced very gravely, 'A second doctor is wanted.' The lecture went on in deeper silence than ever. All the audience were waiting for a third announcement. It came. A new message was handed to the chairman. He rose and said, 'If Mr. Murchison, the undertaker, is in the audience, will he kindly step outside.'

That man, I regret to say, got well. (MDE 166–7)

The chairman rises. He doesn't call for silence. It is there, thick. 'We have with us tonight,' he says, 'a man whose name is well known to the Philosophical Society' (*here he looks at his card*), 'Mr. Stephen Leacock.' (*Complete Silence.*) 'He is a professor of political economy at – ' Here he turns to me and says, 'Which college did you say?' I answer quite audibly in the silence, 'At McGill.' 'He is at McGill,' says the chairman (*More silence.*) 'I don't suppose, however, ladies and gentlemen, that he's come here to talk about political economy.' This is meant as a jest, but the audience takes it as a threat. 'However, ladies and gentlemen, you haven't come here to listen to me' (*this evokes applause, the first of the evening*), 'so without more ado' (*the man always has the impression that there's been a lot of 'ado,' but I never see any of it*) 'I'll now introduce Mr. Leacock.' (*Complete silence.*) (MDE 177)

I find, for example, that wherever I go there is always seated in the audience, about three seats from the front, a silent man with a big motionless face like a melon. He is always there. I have seen that man in every city from Richmond, Indiana, to Bournemouth in Hampshire. He haunts me. I get to expect him. I feel like nodding to him from the platform. And I find that all other lecturers have the same experience. Wherever they go a man with the big face is always there. He never laughs; no matter if the people all round him are convulsed with laughter, he sits there like a rock – or, no, like a

toad – immovable. What he thinks I don't know. Why he comes to
lectures I cannot guess. Once, and once only, I spoke to him, or
rather, he spoke to me. I was coming out from the lecture and found
myself close to him in the corridor. It had been a rather gloomy
evening; the audience had hardly laughed at all; and I know nothing
sadder than a humorous lecture without laughter. The man with the
big face, finding himself beside me, turned and said, 'Some of them
people weren't getting that tonight.' His tone of sympathy seemed to
imply that he had got it *all* himself; if so, he must have swallowed it
whole without a sign. But I have since thought that this man with
the big face may have his own internal form of appreciation. This
much, however, I know: to look at him from the platform is fatal.
One sustained look into his big, motionless face and the lecturer
would be lost; inspiration would die upon one's lips – the basilisk
isn't in it with him.

Personally, I no sooner see the man with the big face than instinctively I turn my eyes away. I look round the hall for another man
that I know is always there, the opposite type, the little man with
the spectacles. There he sits, good soul, about twelve rows back, his
large spectacles beaming with appreciation and his quick face antici-
pating every point. I imagine him to be by trade a minor journalist
or himself a writer of sorts, but with not enough of success to have
spoiled him.

There are other people always there, too. There is the old lady
who thinks the lecture improper; it doesn't matter how moral it is,
she's out for impropriety and she can find it anywhere. Then there is
another very terrible man against whom American lecturers in
England should be warned – the man who is leaving on the 9 p.m.
train. English railways running into suburbs and nearby towns have
a schedule which is expressly arranged to have the principal train
leave before the lecture ends. Hence the 9-p.m.-train man. He sits
right near the front, and at ten minutes to nine he gathers up his
hat, coat, and umbrella very deliberately, rises with great calm, and
walks firmly away. His air is that of a man who has stood all that he

can and can bear no more. Till one knows about this man, and the others who rise after him, it is very disconcerting; at first I thought I must have said something to reflect upon the royal family. But presently the lecturer gets to understand that it is only the nine o'clock train and that all the audience know about it. Then it's all right. It's just like the people rising and stretching themselves after the seventh innings in baseball. (MDE 181–2)

That's all the lecture. Those still here had better go soon, as the light will be put out. You can find some other place to sit just as warm. Good night. Good-bye. (HML 167)

BUSINESS

When the business man is busy with the buzzing of his brain
And his mind is set on bonds and stocks and shares,
While he's building up the country with his utmost might and
    main,
Do you think it's for the country that he cares?

When he's making us a railroad, when he's digging us a mine
Every philanthropic benefit he flaunts,
When he says that he has blest us with his output of asbestos,
It is nothing but our money that he wants. (CoD 127–8)

The Business Man, to the ancient Greeks and Romans, was a crook.
To the Middle Ages he was a sinner. In the polite world of Queen
Anne and the Georges he had turned into a Merchant, but even
then gentlemen did not eat with him – except at his expense.
(HML 234)

They were both what we commonly call successful business-men –
men with well-fed faces, heavy signet rings on fingers like sausages,
and broad, comfortable waistcoats, a yard and a half round the
equator. (LL 114)

Any man can think and think hard when he has to: the savage devotes a nicety of thought to the equipoise of his club, or the business man to the adjustment of a market price. (ELS 19)

A trustee, according to the old-fashioned Victorian novels, was a man to whom no one should ever have entrusted a shilling. (OPM 7)

Everything with us is 'run' on business lines from a primary election to a prayer meeting. Thus business, and the business code, and business principles become everything. Smartness is the quality most desired, pecuniary success the goal to be achieved. Hence all less tangible and provable forms of human merit, and less tangible aspirations of the human mind are rudely shouldered aside by business ability and commercial success. There follows the apotheosis of the business man. He is elevated to the post of national hero. (ELS 92–3)

So it came about that success and the generosity of the Business Man led to a glorification that amounted to Apotheosis. For every social purpose it seemed that what was needed was a committee of Business Men. Was there a city to be saved? Get a committee of Business men! A maternity hospital to be developed? Leave it to the Business Men. A couple of religions to be amalgamated? Let a committee of Business Men do it; they're used to it.

In return the Business Man asked nothing from the colleges and the colleges gave him nothing – apart from the letters of a degree, by accepting which he kindly uplifted all those beneath him. There was nothing they could give him. Masses for his soul? What an idea! As if a man as smart as that would be caught with a soul. (HML 235–6)

The other day I had a few minutes' conversation (I couldn't afford more) with one of the biggest-priced men in this country. 'To what,' I asked, 'do you attribute your own greatness?' He answered without hesitation, 'To myself.'

Yet this was a man who has the reputation of being the second biggest consumer of crude rubber in this country. He may do it and he may not, but he has that reputation. I asked another man, a large consumer of adjustable bicycle parts, how much he thought he owed of his present commanding position to education. He answered emphatically, 'Nothing.' Something in his tone made me believe him.

Now the common element in all these men is personality. Each one of them has a developed, balanced, nicely adjusted well-hung personality. You feel that as soon as such a man is in your presence; when he enters a room, you are somehow aware that he has come in. When he leaves, you realize that he has gone out. As soon as he opens his mouth, you know that he is speaking. When he shuts his mouth, you feel that he has stopped.

Until the recent discoveries of the success movement it was not known that personality could be acquired. We know now that it can.

For the acquirement of personality, the first thing needed is *to get into harmony with yourself.* You may think that this is difficult. But a little practice will soon show you how. Make the effort, so far as you can, to set up a *bilateral harmony between your inner and your outer ego.* When you get this done start and see what you can do to *extend yourself in all directions.* This is a little hard at first, but the very difficulty will lend zest to the effort. As soon as you begin to feel that you are doing it, then try, gently at first, but with increasing emphasis, to *revolve about your own axis.* When you have got this working nicely, slowly and carefully at first, *lift yourself to a new level of thinking.* When you have got up there, hold it.

(GF 15–16)

It's all right to talk about education and that sort of thing, but if you want driving power and efficiency, get business men. They're seeing it every day in the city, and it's just the same in Mariposa. Why, in the big concerns in the city, if they found out a man was educated, they wouldn't have him, – wouldn't keep him there a minute. That's why the business men have to conceal it so much. (SS 69)

∽

'The face,' so wrote the editor of the 'Our Own Men' section of *Ourselves Monthly*, 'is that of a typical American captain of finance, hard, yet with a certain softness, broad but with a certain length, ductile but not without its own firmness.'

'The mouth,' so wrote the editor of the 'Success' column of *Brains*, 'is strong but pliable, the jaw firm and yet movable, while there is something in the set of the ear that suggests the swift, eager mind of the born leader of men.' (AA 24)

∽

Alert, keen, with every faculty awake – with a figure as erect at fifty as at twenty-five – the [Shucksford College] president's appearance was that of the ideal money-getter. There was something in the firmness of his face and in his keen intelligent eye which suggested the getting of money, while his long prehensile hand, with every finger joint working to perfection, suggested the keeping, or retention of it. (AU 153)

∽

He was a man of many activities; president and managing director of the companies just mentioned, trustee and secretary of St. Asaph's, honorary treasurer of the university, etc.: and each of his occupations and offices was marked by something of a supramundane character, something higher than ordinary business. His different official positions naturally overlapped and brought him into contact with himself from a variety of angles. (AA 110)

The Overend brothers, who were Tom's uncles (his name being Tom Overend) were, as everybody knew, among the principal supporters of St. Osoph's. Not that they were, by origin, Presbyterians. But they were self-made men, which put them once and for all out of sympathy with such a place as St. Asaph's [Episcopalian]. 'We made ourselves,' the two brothers used to repeat in defiance of the catechism of the Anglican Church. They never wearied of explaining how Mr. Dick, the senior brother, had worked overtime by day to send Mr. George, the junior brother, to school by night, and how Mr. George had then worked overtime by night to send Mr. Dick to school by day. Thus they had come up the business ladder hand over hand, landing later on in life on the platform of success like two corpulent acrobats, panting with the strain of it. 'For years,' Mr. George would explain, 'we had father and mother to keep as well; then they died, and Dick and me saw daylight.' (AA 111)

Another guest appeared to answer to the general designation of Capitalist or Philanthropist, and seemed from his prehensile grasp upon his knife and fork to typify the Money Power. In front of this guest, doubtless with a view of indicating his extreme wealth and the consideration in which he stood, was placed a floral decoration representing a broken bank, with the figure of a ruined depositor entwined among the debris. (FF 133)

In short they were a typical group of what are now called 'big' men – men who do 'big' things. They were not 'thinkers.' They were men who don't need to think. So it is naturally most impressive to hear these men say that they had never done fractions in their lives. If big men like them have no use for fractions what earthly good are fractions anyway? (GF 162–3)

The world's knowledge is thus reduced to a very short compass. But I doubt if even now it is sufficiently concentrated. Even the briefest outlines yet produced are too long for the modern business man. We have to remember that the man is busy. And when not busy he is tired. He has no time to go wading through five whole pages of print just to find out when Greece rose and fell. It has got to fall quicker than that if it wants to reach him. As to reading up a long account, with diagrams, of how the protozoa differentiated itself during the twenty million years of the Pleistocene era into the first invertebrate, the thing is out of the question. The man hasn't got twenty million years. The whole process is too long. We need something shorter, snappier, something that brings more immediate results. (WW 2)

The light emitted from these stars comes from distances so vast that most of it is not here yet. But owing to the great distance involved the light from the stars is of no commercial value. One has only to stand and look up at the sky on a clear starlight night to realize that the stars are of no use. (WW 11)

I find that the men who can sell me encyclopedias are the men who suggest that there is some strange, mysterious purpose in their personality. Such a man looks at me with penetrating power and says in a voice that Forbes Robertson might envy, 'I have here an encyclopedia,' – and when he says it that way I am sunk.

It is just the same idea as with the Ancient Mariner, when he stopped the stranger and held him back even on his way to a wedding feast.

He holds him with his skinny hand,
He holds him with his glittering eye.

Now, that ancient mariner if he went 'on the road' would be worth fifty dollars a day. (SC 87–8)

∞

I don't know who started this ['caring' advertising]. I suppose in a sense we are all brothers. So are the monkeys. But the plain truth is that when a man is doing business, he is not trying to be a brother to anybody – except to himself. (SC 88)

∞

I want to express my opinion right here and now to the reading public that there is getting to be far too much of this 'heart-to-heart,' 'brother-brother,' 'service' stuff in the world to-day [ca. 1929]. I refer to all sorts of letters, circulars, communications – everybody knows just the kind of stuff I mean.

Who writes it, and just why they write it, I don't know. Some of them, I imagine, mistake it for 'efficiency'; some of them are just a little soft in the head, and some of them, more likely still, are just the sort of low-down pups who would really write it. (IM 257)

∞

The trouble with these brother-brother people is that they disfigure the whole of life with the pretence of sentiments that they don't feel. Life is not all brotherhood or service – at least not outside of Salt Lake City. Business is business; has been, and always will be. Part of it is hard; but it is not made softer by throwing over it a whitewash of hypocrisy. ...

I suppose they wouldn't write this kind of stuff unless there were some people to be misled by it. It is quite possible that the human brain is diminishing in size and is softening in texture. That may account for it. Many things of this sort make people of my age [sixty] almost anxious to finish with this world and start off for another. (IM 261–2)

⁓

Little children reading history often wonder how the King could behead the meek old men. Wiser people knew then, and know now, that very often meek old men need beheading the worst way. The man who orders it was called a 'tyrant' in Greece, a 'dictator' in Rome, a 'despotic monarch' in Tudor times, and today a 'business executive.' (MDW 211)

⁓

Advertising may be described as the science of arresting the human intelligence long enough to get money from it. (GF 123)

CANADA

The name 'Canada' used to be just as bad [as 'Britain'] but is now pretty well straightened out. Nobody knows where it came from. When Jacques Cartier came up the St. Lawrence in 1535 on his way to McGill University (then called Hochelaga), he came to the great river that we call Saguenay – in fact, the Indians told him that up this and beyond it, farther west, was the Kingdom of Saguenay, full of gold and diamonds; they were right in a way. Savage legend always has a background. They meant the Hollinger mine, and God's Lake and Flin-Flon, the legend of gold and silver beyond the divide, which later turned out to be true. But they told Cartier, also, that if he went on up the river he would come to 'Canada,' and when he got to where Quebec is they said, 'This is Canada and beyond it is Hochelaga' (corner of McGill College Avenue and Burnside) ... What did the name mean? We don't know. Some said it was Algonquin *Kanata* – a collection of wigwams. Later some one made a joke, 'It's Spanish Aca-Nada' – meaning 'nothing there.' That joke got into the schoolbooks of my youth as dead earnest (the education department in Ontario was Scotch) and stayed there. (LaL 64)

The only trouble for us Canadian lies in the words 'honestly and properly.' We no sooner see government money in sight than we line up in sections, with local interest everywhere clamorous. Worse than that, if one may say it very gently, in dealing with government money we are individually not just quite exactly what you'd call honest. In our private lives we are straight as a string. We wouldn't cheat a bar-tender out of a nickel. We can sit down to a game of poker and never use more than four aces. We wouldn't give a lead quarter to a taxi-man. But let us deal with the Government, and this is different. We have somehow grown up with the idea that the Government is there to be cheated, that, of course, it must pay too much, get too little, expropriate high and sell low. (MDW 36)

∽

In summarizing and judging the existing situation, one may say, first, that in all these matters of the disputes, denunciations and recriminations of parties, it is better for us in Canada if we try not to denounce but to comprehend. (MDW 125)

∽

From this joint heritage [of French, Scotch, and Métis in Manitoba] the course of history dispossessed them. The flood of Ontario settlers broke in on them. The Americans invaded them. Last of all, polyglot Europe washed over them, – much of it not even washed. Can one wonder that the French feel, one must not say a bitterness, but a wistful regret for their lost North West. And suppose we had had it and shared it on equal terms, with a bi-lingual culture to match the older East, it might seem perhaps a more balanced Canada, a more real unity.

It is strange what a queer touchiness surrounds the whole question of bi-lingualism in Canada. It shows how easily decent people can dispute among themselves over nothing. In the early spring of the present year [1937] quite a storm arose in the Canadian tea-cup when the gallant and distinguished English-Canadian at the head of our Broadcast Corporation, expressed his warm appreciation of our dual heritage and used the wrong phrase to express it. The Ontario members of parliament understood him to mean that he was going to teach them to speak French. The Leader of the Opposition quite rightly protested that he couldn't do it. I know he was right because there are members now in the House to whom I tried to teach French at Upper Canada College forty years ago, and who can't speak it yet. (MDW 156–7)

The demand [ca. 1937] is for further separatism, for the breaking of the union, or the imposition of new terms as the price of consenting to stay in. The sorrows of the Maritimes are too well known to need rehearsal. But now comes the demand for secession in the very heart of French Canada, – the parent home of our commonwealth. It is as if the nest wanted to leave the young birds, the old homestead to get up and walk away. It seems incredible but a lot of younger French-Canadians talk now of 'Laurentia,' – a republic on the St. Lawrence. It is a dream that vanishes on waking, a bubble that bursts at a touch. How could French Canada secede without Montreal? Does Laurentia take with it the English banks and magnates and Mc-Gill University with its professors, both active and super-active? Will the Republic hold and control the St. Lawrence, dictating to 125,000,000 other people? Or will Laurentia put on the old-time mantle of poverty and devotion and retire to the snows of the Peribonka, in the land of Maria Chapdelaine? (MDW 218)

When I write about the North I speak with a certain authority. For I know the North, as few people know it. In the corporeal, bodily sense, I have never been there. But in my arm chair, in front of the fire in my house on Cote des Neiges Road in Montreal, I have traversed it all, from the portages back of Lake Superior to where the Mackenzie delta washes into the tidal seas. I have been with Franklin on the Coppermine and Coronation Gulf, with Hudson till I lost him owing to his own folly, with Mackenzie over the divide, in Red River ox-carts with Butler, and in the foothills with Milton and Cheadle. In the snow-storms and Arctic blizzards I feel perfectly at home; if it gets really bad I just lie down in the snow, along with Stefansson, and let it bury me completely and lie there for a day or two and read a book till it moderates. But I must say I don't think I ever felt such intense cold as on crossing the Coppermine running hard with ice through barren treeless country of slate and stone. Imagine trusting oneself on a river like that on a sort of raft or boat made of willow sticks, wet to the skin, in piercing cold. I had to get up and mix a hot whisky and stir the fire and leave Franklin and Richardson to freeze awhile till I rejoined them. (MDW 248–9)

There is not as yet [ca. 1941] a Canadian literature in the sense indicated. Nor is there similarly a Canadian humour, nor any particularly Canadian way of being funny. Nor is there, apart from varying accents, any Canadian language. We use English for writing, American for conversation and slang and profanity, and Scottish models for moral philosophy and solemnity. (CFF 215)

I myself talk Ontario English; I don't admire it, but it's all I can do; anything is better than affectation. (HTW 121)

CAN-AM RELATIONS

It may be well to remind the reader at the outset of this article that Canada is in America. ... Canadian literature, – as far as there is such a thing [ca. 1916], – Canadian journalism, and the education and culture of the mass of the people of Canada approximates more nearly to the type and standard of the United States than to those of Great Britain ... This modest apology may fittingly be offered before throwing stones at the glass house in which both the Canadian and the Americans proper dwell. (ELS 65–6)

We have long since decided that politically our ways lie separate, but the very fixity of that resolve makes it easier and better and finer for us to let our ways mingle as closely as ever they possibly can. (HML 26)

The Canadian Parliament is opening up a debate on imperial and national defense [ca. 1937]. It is a dangerous discussion. The attempt to show that we need to join in Empire defense may lead people to pretend that we need defense here, as against the Americans.

That is just crazy and worse. That could do infinite harm. Our best defense, our only defense, against the Americans, and theirs against us, is to have no defense at all. None that either of us could ever prepare would be effective along such a frontier. We live in peace or die together.

We show every sign of living in peace. Don't let's spoil it by pretending that we need air-bases and gas masks and sally ports and demi-culverins and half-scotches against the Americans. We don't. Honestly, I wouldn't shoot an American, even if I found him sitting on a bough where I could sneak right up on him. (MDW 88–9)

∽

Annexation to the United States! What a strange part that idea, that phrase, has played in our history and how completely it has passed out of it [ca. 1944]. It has served as a sort of bogey or warning – just as children are told that the Devil will get them if they're not good. (LaL 146–7)

∽

By an odd chance the forty-ninth parallel, an astronomical line, turned out to mean something. From Lake Superior to Manitoba the physical separation of the two countries is very real. Manitoba itself is an exception as the valley of the Red River presents a single and unified geography that makes Manitoba and Minnesota one. If steamboat days had lasted one could have imagined a dense, intermingled settlement making the two countries indistinguishable. (MDW 163–4)

∽

But after all what does the 'Americanization' talk amount to? Every now and then – and again quite recently [ca. 1937] – English newspapers break out into a discussion of what is called the 'Americanization of Canada.' The basis of the discussion is always a sort of underlying fear that Canada is getting a little too close to the United States. It is the same sort of apprehension as is felt on a respectable farm when the daughter of the family is going out too much with the hired man. The idea is that you can't tell what might happen.

In the case of Canada, the danger symptoms of what may happen are supposed to be that Canada is 'flooded' with American newspapers and magazines; that Canada is 'deluged' with American broadcasts, 'saturated' with American tourists, and 'permeated' with American ideas; that American tourists cross the border in an unending stream, and Canadian tourists go back with them like a receding tide; that conventions and reunions assemble indifferently on either side of the line; that education is almost indistinguishable as carried on at Harvard or at Toronto. All these things, and a hundred more, are produced as a terrible warning of what may follow next – the handwriting on the wall that signifies that our Belshazzar's Feast of Friendship is nearly at an end. In other words, a relationship which should stand as a bright and conspicuous example for less fortunate nations, as an ideal and hope for distracted Europe, is turned against us as a mark of under-patriotism and lack of national spirit. ...

That this relationship is likely to end in, or even move towards, a political union, is just a forgotten dream. For those of us who best know this North American continent, on both sides of the line, know also that there is not on the present horizon, nor in the furthest vision possible, any prospect of a political amalgamation of the two countries.

The truth is that what we have in Canada and the United States is what all the world must get or perish. It is universal peace or nothing. (MDW 166–8)

⁂

The carp itself, the very fish which *The Compleat Angler* helps us to turn into a dainty dish, is very commonly thrown away with us in Canada as worthless – or else, if I may say it without offence, exported to the United States. (LaL 19)

⁂

Indeed, if any one wants to understand our relations with one another better than history can tell or statistics teach, let him go and stand anywhere along the Niagara-Buffalo frontier at holiday time –

fourth of July or first of July, either one – they're all one to us [ca. 1944]. Here are the Stars and Stripes and the Union Jacks all mixed up together and the tourists pouring back and forward over the International Bridge; immigration men trying in vain to sort them out; Niagara mingling its American and Canadian waters and its honeymoon couples ... Or go to the Detroit-Windsor frontier and move back and forward with the flood of commuters, of Americans sampling ale in Windsor and Canadians sampling lager in Detroit ... or come here to Montreal and meet the Dartmouth boys playing hockey against McGill ... or if that sounds too cold, come to Lake Memphremagog in July and go out bass fishing and hook up the International Boundary itself.

But all such fraternization is only all the more fraternal because we know that we are satisfied on each side of the line to keep our political systems different. (LaL 151)

CANADIAN CITIES

I pulled up the blind and looked out of the window and there was the good old city [Toronto ca. 1919], with the bright sun sparkling on its church spires and on the bay spread out at its feet. It looked quite unchanged: just the same pleasant old place, as cheerful, as self-conceited, as kindly, as hospitable, as quarrelsome, as wholesome, as moral and as loyal and as disagreeable as it always was. (FrF 147)

So what they are saying over in England is that rebuilding the cities [post-WWII] will involve a lot of inner-city housing for those who won't go out. This, I think, is true; it's like being Liberals and Conservatives; people are just that way and can't help it. This question of inner-city versus outer will vary very much from city to city, especially according to climate. In Toronto, people will want to get out as far as they can; in Montreal, they will want to stick inside. They always have. (LaL 85–6)

As a matter of fact, a full mastery of even two languages is a very rare thing. It can only come as the result of a special environment, the opportunity to talk both, the will to do so, and therewith a certain aptitude. What is ordinarily thought as bilingualism falls away below this.

Compare, for example, the 'bilingual' city of Montreal [ca. 1939], of whose one million people, some seven out of ten are French. All the French people of any education understand English, and all of them speak it in a way to make themselves easily understood for business and for ordinary conversation. But with a very few exceptions their speech falls far short of the range and power of people speaking their own language. They can say what they mean but they can neither adorn nor embellish it. ...

As to the bilingualism of the English people of Montreal there is hardly any of it. Most of them learn a little French in school, recognize a lot of French words, especially those on sign-boards and know that 'Guy Street!' as called out by the bilingual car-conductor is in French 'Ghee!' The exceptions are too few to matter. Yet here is a city where an unobservant visitor, haunted by a myth, would say, 'In Montreal, of course, everybody talks both English and French.' (TMC 104–5)

Lord Nosh was the perfect type of the English nobleman and statesman. The years that he had spend in the diplomatic service at Constantinople, St. Petersburg, and Salt Lake City had given to him a peculiar finesse and noblesse, while his long residence at St. Helena, Pitcairn Island, and Hamilton, Ontario, had rendered him impervious to external impressions. (NN 58–9)

A great American banker, speaking the other day in Saskatoon, Saskatchewan (it was not his fault) ... (SC 80)

Foreign words were now and then dropped on to our map without trace of origin; as witness the Spanish 'Orillia' that fell mercifully out of the sky as an improvement over Champlain's 'Cahigué.' (CFF 36)

The scale of the emptiness and the openness of Fort William [Thunder Bay] makes New York and London seem crowded, breathless anthills, – no place for *men*. I'd like to live there. I'd like to go to Fort William young and live there fifty years till it had five hundred thousand inhabitants, and get old and half childish and prattle away about what it was like when it only had fifty thousand. (MDW 10).

❧

Those who love Winnipeg, – and they all do, – explain that though it is cold it is 'dry,' and that being dry, you don't feel the cold. People always defend their home town in this way: London explains away its fog, Pittsburgh its smoke and Aberdeen its rain. It appears that the fog is not fog at all but *mist*, that the smoke is only *carbon*, and that the rain isn't really wet. So with the pleas that Winnipeg is 'dry.' It may be. I saw no sign of it while I was there, – it seemed, – indoors anyway, – wetter than Aberdeen.

More than that, – the place is not only cold, it's drafty. It has the two widest streets of any capital city in the world, – Main Street and Portage Avenue, – but even they can't hold all the wind. With the thermometer at 30 below zero, and the wind behind him, a man walking on Main Street, Winnipeg, knows which side of him is which. (MDW 39)

❧

One last feature remains to record and to commend in the Winnipeg of the bye-gone days, – a feature that left upon it a mark that it still wears. This is the cosmopolitan, world-wide outlook of Winnipeg, that shows itself in the city press, in the public organisations and in the university and learned societies. The city runs true to its first form. It was from its birth a cosmopolitan place, a meeting place of people from all over the world. It was born, so to speak, into the sunlight of the larger world, and had nothing of the long slow twilight of the growth of other cities. George Grant, the later principal of Queen's, noticed this when he visited the place for the second time, in 1881. 'Winnipeg,' he said, 'is London or New York on a small scale. You meet people from all over the world.' A result of this was the appearance in the little town of almost every known form of institution and patriotic society, a historical club, a St. Andrew's society, with another society for St. George and one for St. Patrick. The whole social life was buttressed, perhaps stimulated, with a supply of saloons that attracted the notice of every visitor.

Winnipeg, like the rest of us, was born in mingled sin and righteousness. Purged now of its sin, it keeps the virtue of its cosmopolitan outlook. Buried in the heart of a continent, it still looks over the rim of it in all directions. (MDW 52–3)

Vancouver is a wonder city [ca. 1937]. There will be a million people in it in twenty years. It has the combined excellence of nature's gift and man's handiwork. God did a lot for Montreal, but man didn't add to it. Quebec is historical and has a majesty of situation, but a lot of it is squalid: Toronto, – I come from there myself, so I have the right to insult it, – Toronto is a village and always will be, if it spreads out a hundred miles wide: the prairie cities are impressive in their isolation and extension – fill in houses and they will be wonderful – but Vancouver is wonderful right now ... 'If I had known what it [British Columbia] was like,' I said, 'I wouldn't have been content with a mere visit. I'd have been born here.' (MDW 172–3)

But as I was saying, Vancouver Island with the city of Victoria that lies at the foot of it, represents the last word in charm of climate and in beauty. Beyond it, till we reach another world, is nothing. Here is the long slow spring of England, lingering over its early flowers: here the wet tears of April sunshine weeping for a winter that never was; a luxuriant summer that blossoms but never burns; autumn mellow with mist and fruit; and well in time to make an English Christmas, a mimic winter, with a tang of frost in the air, a make believe snowstorm, with angry threatenings that dissolve again into sunshine.

Such a Christmas and such a winter as a Charles Dickens might love, a truly Pickwickian season. (MDW 193–4)

The residents of Victoria wake up in the morning, roll over, read the obituary columns, and if they're not listed, go back to sleep. (Attributed)

CANADIAN POLITICS

Harsh is the cackle of the little turkey-cocks of Ottawa, fighting the while as they feather their mean nests of sticks and mud, high on their river bluff. Loud sings the Little Man of the Province, crying his petty Gospel of Provincial Rights, grudging the gift of power, till the cry spreads and town hates town and every hamlet of the country side shouts for its share of plunder and pelf. (GCA 136)

Government, and ours at Ottawa especially, for we live in peace, is apt to grow complacent in office: alternating from a decorous ministry to a decorous opposition, keeping the tariff, and the annual deficit, and the railway muddle as a joint heritage of stock-in-trade: soothing as best they may the sobs of the Maritimes, tabulating the weather, taking holidays at Geneva, and holding, every now and then, a Royal Commission on the Solar System. Would that such halcyon days were forever possible! (MDW 131)

Bagshaw of Mariposa was one of the most representative men of the age, and it's no wonder that he had been returned for the county for five elections running, leaving the Conservatives nowhere. Just think how representative he was. He owned two hundred acres out on the Third Concession and kept two men working on it all the time to prove that he was a practical farmer. They sent in fat hogs to the Missinaba County Agricultural Exposition and the World's Fair every autumn, and Bagshaw himself stood beside the pig pens with the judges, and wore a pair of corduroy breeches and chewed a straw all afternoon. After that if any farmer thought that he was not properly represented in Parliament, it showed that he was an ass.

Bagshaw owned a half share in the harness business and quarter share in the tannery and that made him a business man. He paid for a pew in the Presbyterian Church and that represented religion in Parliament. He attended college for two sessions thirty years ago, and that represented education and kept him abreast with modern science, if not ahead of it. He kept a little account in one bank and a big account in the other, so that he was a rich man or a poor man at the same time. (SS 123)

At home in Canada our politics turn on such things as how much money the Canadian National Railways lose as compared with how much they could lose if they really tried; on whether the Grain Growers of Manitoba should be allowed to import ploughs without paying a duty or to pay a duty without importing the ploughs. (MDE 60–1)

In every great movement that enlists the sympathy of thousands of disinterested persons there must be an element of right. So it must be, not with Social Credit, but with the Social Credit movement in the West [ca. 1937]. Social Credit in the sense of economic theory is mere wind, words and nothing else. It creates a vague ideal of 'purchasing power' and wishes that everybody might have lots of it. So do I. I'd buy a new Fedora hat with it this morning. The demand that 'purchasing power' must be given to the people means nothing more than that the people ought to be better off, and that society is all wrong till they are. All sensible people think that. But there is no way to make an act of legislature to sprinkle all the people with 'purchasing power' as you sprinkle a lawn with a hose. (MDW 125–6)

At the same time it is altogether likely that a 'Social Credit party' is here to stay, at least for some time. It will be a people's party of radical reform, having about as much to do with social credit as the Liberal part has to do with liberalism, or the Conservative party with conservatism. This is always the way with parties. 'Socialist parties' become bourgeois as they have in France [ca. 1937], 'labour parties' quit work and wear evening dress and 'clerical parties' go to the devil. (MDW 135–6)

In all institutions, in all laws, the inspiring spirit must come first. Legislation is worthless except as it expresses a purpose already there. People cannot be made virtuous by act of parliament, honest by an order-in-council, or sober by a municipal by-law. It is the fault of younger people, especially of academic people, to think that society can be made and fashioned by law. It is part of the very innocence of their optimism. Laws merely express and make regular the forces that the mind and will of society have already brought into being. It is because people are determined not to steal that we have laws against burglary. The burglar is the odd man out. He is the exception that proves the rule.

What we need to do, therefore, in Canada for our salvation is, first of all, to renew a right heart and spirit within us. We need first of all an ardent purpose to make things better. (MDW 255)

CANADIAN PROVINCES

I am also credibly informed that the theological essayists of Prince Edward Island challenge comparison with those of any age. It is no doubt not the fault of the Islanders that this challenge has not yet been accepted. (ELS 67)

They're strong on divinity. You have to be in a country as bleak as the Nova Scotia coast. (LaL 143)

But human kind in the West before the white man came to America must have been infinitely rare, as far as the vast open prairie was concerned. Men couldn't live there. Not till the Spaniards brought the horse to America, and the wild horses multiplied, could mankind invade, in any real fashion, the open plains; and even then rather in annual raids and inroads than in fixed settlement. This was the 'buffalo and hunters' stage; the lost paradise of the half breed living under the rule of the great Company. Then came the settler to the plains, with his acquired apparatus of civilization and his mechanism of agriculture. The Company rule ended, the homestead farmers invaded the West. The Lord said 'let there be wheat' and Saskatchewan was born. (MDW 73)

Incidentally I may say that I had personal opportunities while I was in England of realizing that the reputation of the *Times* staff for the possession of information is well founded. Dining one night with some members of the staff, I happened to mention Saskatchewan. One of the editors at the other end of the table looked up at the mention of the name. 'Saskatchewan,' he said, 'ah, yes; that's not far from Alberta, is it?' and then turned quietly to his food again. When I remind the reader that Saskatchewan is only half an inch from Alberta he may judge of the nicety of the knowledge involved. (MDE 113)

MUSSOLINI VISITS OTTAWA

OTTAWA, Wednesday. – Signor Mussolini yesterday paid a flying visit to Ottawa [ca. 1928] with a view to seeing how much of the government would need to be abolished at once and how much of it might be left over till next year. He expressed his regret that the Prime Minister is not wearing a black shirt and offered to lend him his other one. It is said that Mussolini will very likely advocate the entire abolition of the Prairie Provinces. (SC 126)

What will happen is probably this [ca. 1937]. The sunshine will break out again over sunny Alberta. The wheat will wave and the price will jump. Of course the Dominion will lend money, – Ottawa was never cruel, – and anyway if it is true that the province doesn't need it, then they are just the people to lend it to. The Commission will report on Social Credit, – say half a million words. No one will read it because on the day it comes out there'll be a ball-game between Edmonton and Lethbridge, or a stampede at Calgary, or a three-headed calf born at Wetaskiwin and Social Credit will be off the front page. (MDW 134)

That's the great thing about the Prairies, the colder it is outside, the warmer it is in the human heart. Don't talk to me of languid audiences in the tropics, sticky with heat and faint with saturation. You couldn't knock a laugh out of them with a hockey stick. But let me have the Quota Club of Medicine Hat, or the Wives and Mothers of Regina, or the Old Boys of Anything (a pretty young crowd) at Edmonton or Saskatoon, – with 20 or 30 below outside and the snow against the hotel windows! – and you've a grand start towards a big evening if you don't spoil it yourself. (MDW 260)

CRITICS

Modern critics, who refuse to let a plain thing alone, have now started a theory that Cervantes's work is a vast piece of 'symbolism.' If so, Cervantes didn't know it himself and nobody thought of it for three hundred years. He meant it as a satire upon the silly romances of chivalry. (HH 129)

The classical scholars have kept alive the tradition of the superiority of the ancient languages – a kaleidoscopic mass of suffixes and prefixes, supposed to represent an infinite shading of meaning. It is a character that they share with the Ojibway and the Zulu. (HTT 242)

But as the modern parent [ca. 1928] and the modern teacher have grown alarmed, the art of story-telling for children has got to be softened down. There must be no more horror and blood and violent death. Away with the giants and the ogres! Let us have instead the stories of the animal kingdom in which Wee-Wee the Mouse has tea on a broad leaf with Goo-goo the Caterpillar, and in which Fuzzy the Skunk gives talks on animal life that would do for Zoölogy Class I at Harvard.

But do we – do they – can we escape after all from the cruel environment that makes up the life in which we live? Are the animals after all so much softer than the ogres, so much kinder than the pirates? When Slick the Cat crackles up the bones of Wee-Wee the

Mouse, how does that stand! And when old Mr. Hawk hovers in the air watching for Cheep-cheep the chicken who tries in vain to hide under the grass, and calls for its lost mother – how is that for terror! To my thinking the timorous and imaginative child can get more real terror from the pictured anguish of a hunted animal than from the deaths of all the Welsh giants that ever lived on Plynlimmon.

The tears of childhood fall fast and easily, and evil be to him who makes them flow.

How easily a child will cry over the story of a little boy lost, how easily at the tale of poverty and want, how inconsolably at death. Touch but ever so lightly these real springs of anguish and the ready tears will come. But at Red Riding Hood's grandmother! Never! She didn't *die*! She was merely *eaten*. And the sailors, and the pirates, and the Apache Indians! They don't *die*, not in any real sense to the child. They are merely 'swept off,' and 'mowed down' – in fact, scattered like the pieces on an upset chessboard. The moral of all which is, don't worry about the apparent terror and bloodshed in the children's books, the real children's books. There is none there. It only represents the way in which little children, from generation to generation, learn in ways as painless as can be followed, the stern environment of life and death. (SC 202–3)

෴

An English reviewer writing in a literary journal, the very name of which is enough to put contradiction to sleep, has said of my writing, 'What is there, after all, in Professor Leacock's humour but a rather ingenious mixture of hyperbole and myosis?'

The man was right. How he stumbled upon this trade secret I do not know. But I am willing to admit, since the truth is out, that it has long been my custom in preparing an article of a humorous nature to go down to the cellar and mix up half a gallon of myosis with a pint of hyperbole. If I want to give the article a decidedly literary character, I find it well to put in about half a pint of paresis. The whole thing is amazingly simple. (FF 156–7)

The book's suggestions and proposals may be summarized here [the preface] for readers whose rapid intelligence renders it unnecessary for them to read the book. (BP 101)

In dealing with the mass of statistical material that goes with the making of such a volume as the present [*The British Empire*], it is unavoidable that errors and misprints will find their way in. For these I apologize beforehand. For instance, in Chapter III, I stated that the number of hogs in the world is 200,000,000. I now believe this wrong. There seem to be more than that. Reviewers whose one idea of reviewing is to mop up misprints will add more hogs. (BE v)

Professors of theory merely hold post-mortems. (LaL 67)

DREAMERS

I have always felt that there must be something exhilarating, stimulating, superhuman in the rushing, upward life of a boom town, – A San Francisco of the 50's, a Carson city of the 60's, a Winnipeg of the 80's. The life of the individual fits into the surroundings as into a glove – the 'world' no longer means something far away, something in the papers, – It is right there. In the life of the great cities of today [ca. 1937] the individual is crushed, lost, is nothing. In the boom town his life is life itself. There everybody is somebody. 'Character' springs like a plant and individuality blooms like a rose: and forthwith there are gay people, brave people, and queer people, – room for everybody to be something; not the crushed dead-level uniformity of the metropolis. Everybody becomes, as in Charles Dickens' America, 'a remarkable man': indeed we all are, in reality, if looked into deeply enough. (MDW 49)

It may be those who do most, dream most. (HTW 205)

ECONOMICS

Take enough of that mystification and muddle, combine it with the continental area of the United States, buttress it up on the side with the history of dead opinion and dress it, as the chefs say, with sliced history and green geography, and out of it you can make a doctor's degree in economics. I have one myself. (TMC 120)

The fault with economics was the assumption that what *can only be done by the Spirit* could be done by material interest. (LaL 106)

If the ability to produce goods to meet human wants has multiplied so that each man accomplishes almost thirty or forty times what he did before, then the world at large ought to be about thirty or fifty times better off. But it is not. Or else, as the other possible alternative, the working hours of the world should have been cut down to about one in thirty of what they were before. But they are not. How, then, are we to explain this extraordinary discrepancy between human power and resulting human happiness?

The more we look at our mechanism of production the more perplexing it seems. Suppose an observer were to look down from the cold distance of the moon upon the seething ant-hill of human labor presented on the surface of our globe; and suppose that such an observer knew nothing of our system of individual property, or money payments and wages and contracts, but viewed our labor as merely that of a mass of animated beings trying to supply their wants. The spectacle to his eyes would be strange indeed. Mankind viewed in the mass would be seen to produce a certain amount of absolutely necessary things, such as food, and then to stop. In spite of the fact that there was not food enough to go round, and that large numbers must die of starvation or perish slowly from under-nutrition, the production of food would stop at some point a good deal short of universal satisfaction. So, too, with the production of clothing, shelter and other necessary things; never enough would seem to be produced, and this apparently not by accident or miscalculation, but as if some peculiar social law were at work adjusting production to the point where there is just not enough, and leaving it there. The countless millions of workers would be seen to turn their untired energies and their all-powerful machinery away from the production of necessary things to the making of mere comforts; and from these, again, while still stopping short of a general satisfaction, to the making of luxuries and superfluities. The wheels would never stop. The activity would never tire. Mankind, mad with the energy of activity, would be seen to pursue the fleeing phantom of insatiable desire. Thus among the huge mass of accumulated commodities the simplest want would go unsatisfied. Half-fed men would dig for diamonds, and men sheltered by a crazy roof erect the marble walls of palaces. The observer might well remain perplexed at the pathetic discord between human work and human wants. Something, he would feel assured, must be at fault either with the social instincts of man or with the social order under which he lives. (UR 27–30)

The plain assertion that every man looks out for himself (or at best for himself and his immediate family) touches the tender conscience of humanity. It is an unpalatable truth. None the less it is the most nearly true of all the broad generalizations that can be attempted in regard to mankind. (UR 40)

The fundamental equation of the economist, then, is that the value of everything is proportionate to its cost. It requires no little hardihood to say that this proposition is a fallacy. It lays one open at once, most illogically, to the charge of being a socialist. In sober truth it might as well lay one open to the charge of being an ornithologist. I will not, therefore, say that the proposition that the value of everything equals the cost of production is false. I will say that it is *true*; in fact, that is just as true as that two and two make four: exactly as true as that, but let it be noted most profoundly, *only as true as that*. In other words, it is a truism, mere equation in terms, telling nothing whatever. When I say that two and two make four I find, after deep thought, that I have really said *nothing*, or nothing that was not already said at the moment I defined two and defined four. The new statement that two and two make four adds nothing. So with the majestic equation of the cost of production. It means, as far as social application goes, as far as any moral significance or bearing on social reform and the social outlook goes, *absolutely nothing*. It is not in itself fallacious; how could it be? But all the social inferences drawn from it are absolute, complete and malicious fallacies. (UR 56–7)

Then came the intensification of economic activity called a 'boom' [to Winnipeg in the 1880s]. And the whole thing was sound, absolutely. No wind, no bubble about it; just solid economic fact, that can be repeated over and over again, – on the Peace River, in British Columbia, on Vancouver Island, in Northern Ontario, more or less all over Canada, wherever undeveloped resources, labour, capital and directing brains all come together. We have never understood the nature of a 'boom.' We look at it as a sort of economic fever. Not at all; a 'boom' is a burst of economic health. (MDW 44)

cx/∂

Later on, in the post-war [One] period, something of the same complaint has been raised by the economists. 'The gold standard,' so claims one of the least ignorant (one dare not say *most eminent* of economists), 'is as antiquated as the stage coach.' The metaphor is a favourite one of people without imagination who do not realize that the stage coach was murdered by the railway train and has now come back as its ghost, – the motor car, – to haunt the railway. 'Coaches' blow their horns again from New York to San Francisco and from the Oasis of Timgad to Timbuctoo. But few economists ever had imagination. (MDW 104)

What the London banker and economist and financier mean, if you get down to brass tacks, is that the three of them will 'manage the currency' by themselves in a closed room. If so I'd like to sit in with them and make it four. I'd undertake to come out rich. Talking in ideal terms, 'managed currency' [as opposed to a gold standard] means that all dangerous inflation and credit will be carefully prevented, that dull business will be gradually strengthened, etc., etc. Among a set of omniscient angels, so it would be. With the world as it is, and with us as we are, I don't think it would be. It would just afford a new means in which the organized power of collective finance could act in its own interest. Money must be automatic or nothing. It must be a fact, like a beaver skin, or a roll of tobacco, or a goat, or a bit of paper actually convertible into a bit of metal. (MDW 105–6)

HOW TO MAKE A FORTUNE IN A MERGER

Look carefully all around for two big enterprises that need merging and don't know it. One good way is to get hold of two large railroads and join them into one small one. Another scheme is to go round and gather the whole of an industry into the hollow of your hand and then close it. And another is to lay pipe-lines to carry anything – any sort of product – to where it has never been carried and then open up the top end of the pipe-line.

All these things are so ridiculously and selfishly simple that I share your feeling of indignation against the men who have made colossal fortunes (out of the poor) by doing them. (SC 84–5)

You can never have international peace as long as you have national poverty. (LaL 106)

EDUCATION

The beginning of learning is the urge to learn. The teacher and the class exercise are just a supplement and a help, but never can be the motive power. Wisdom cannot be poured into the pupil out of a jug. (TMC 93–4)

The beginning of learning is the urge to learn. The teacher and the class exercise are just a supplement and a help, but never can be the motive power. Wisdom cannot be poured into the pupil out of a jug. (TMC 93-4)

We are moved and stimulated to understanding far more by our imagination than by our intellect: more even than by our self-interest. (HoH 79)

In my case I went into schoolteaching with my eyes wide open, as into something temporary on the way to a real career. To go into teaching was a matter of sheer necessity. My education had fitted me for nothing except to pass it on to other people. (BLB 154)

Instinctively I went at class order in the right way, and when you know how, it is very simple. It is the beginning which counts. Face the class. Begin talking to them at once. Get to business, not with one of them but with all of them. Talk: don't mumble. Face them: don't turn your back. Start work: don't get fumbling about with a class list of names and a roll call, which you may pronounce correctly or may not. Leave all that till later. Start work, and, once started, they are lost as far as disorder goes. In fact they won't expect any. Above all, don't try to be funny; feeble teachers attempt a footing of fun as a means of getting together. The real teacher descends to fun only when he has established a sufficient height to descend from. (BLB 169–70)

I remember one case in particular of a parent who did not do the boy's exercise but, after letting the boy do it himself, wrote across the face of it a withering comment addressed to me and reading: 'From this exercise you can see that my boy, after six months of your teaching, is completely ignorant. How do you account for it?'

I sent the exercise back to him with the added note: 'I think it must be hereditary.' (CoD 29)

Compulsion has its uses. If a boy learns nothing at school except to keep seated and silent, that in itself is good. We have to be made to do things; our frail human nature otherwise couldn't live up to its own aspirations. Take as a minor instance such a case as compulsory attendance at lectures. Must the student be made to go, and checked off on a list like a factory hand? Yes, I think so. When I first went to teach at McGill, where such a rule was in force, I was horrified at it. I had been used to what seemed the superior liberty of other colleges, seeming more worthy of a man. But in reality students cut lectures from idleness, from whim, or from accident, and later on wish that they had been made to be present. (HML 45)

Teaching, like anything else, is immensely tiring to a novice; later on it gets less and less so in proportion to one's ability to teach. But it is never easy, except to people who can't teach at all or don't try to. (BLB 175)

At the end of his labours he [the graduate student] publishes a useless little pamphlet called his thesis which is new in the sense that nobody ever wrote it before, and erudite in the sense that nobody will ever read it. (ELS 78)

I do not here mean to imply that all our scholars of this type die, or even that they ought to die, immediately after graduation. Many of them remain alive for years, though their utility has of course largely departed after their thesis is complete. Still they do and can remain alive. If kept in a dry atmosphere and not exposed to the light, they may remain in an almost perfect state of preservation for years after finishing their doctor's thesis. (ELS 80)

A college lecture is a queer thing, for people not accustomed to it. The Professor isn't exactly dictating the lecture, and he isn't exactly talking, and the class are not exactly taking dictation and they're not exactly listening. It's a system they both have grown so used to that it's second nature. (HS 13)

We can no longer communicate with the apes by direct language, nor can we understand, without special study, their modes of communication which we have long since replaced by more elaborate forms. But it is at least presumable that they could still detect in our speech, at least when it is public and elaborate, the underlying tone values with which it began. Thus if we could take a gibbon ape to a college public lecture, he would not indeed understand it, but he would 'get a good deal of it.' This is all the students get anyway. (HTW 183–4)

Some years ago I resided for a month or two with a group of men who were specialists of the type described, most of them in pursuit of their degree of Doctor of Philosophy, some of them – easily distinguished by their air of complete vacuity – already in possession of it. The first night I dined with them I addressed to the man opposite me some harmless question about a recent book that I thought of general interest. 'I don't know anything about that,' he answered, 'I'm in sociology.' There was nothing to do but to beg his pardon and to apologise for not having noticed it. (ELS 78–9)

A college is a queer place, full of freak characters and odd activities, with alternating aspects of drowsy inefficiency and alert effectiveness; a queer place, but it gets there just the same. If all the world did its work as well as the college does, then the world, in the words of the old song, 'would do very well then.' (MGC 7–8)

You can't learn a little Greek; it won't divide; it's like a billiard ball. Half of it is no good. (TMC 53)

Hitherto it has been better for the world to pretend that at least somebody could 'read Latin straight off.' Now it is better to have the truth. The Romans themselves couldn't. (TMC 58)

The result, then, of this odd-looking system is, that what ought to be a thing existing for itself is turned into a qualification for something else. ... At the end of [the university student's] course he has learned much. He has learned to sit, – that first requisite for high professional work, – and he can sit for hours. He can write for hours with a stylographic pen: more than that, for I wish to state the case fairly, he can make a digest, or a summary, or a reproduction of anything in the world. Incidentally the *speculation* is all knocked sideways out of him. But the lack of it is never felt. (ELS 22–3)

৵

In my opinion the great majority of the colleges of the United States and Canada contain in their curriculums of liberal arts an accumulation of courses which are little more than an attempt to teach the unteachable; which substitute for the rigour of real study a make-believe activity and a dilettante idleness; which try to make theory out of the commonplace and to turn the obvious into the intricate; which are as pretentious as they are futile and which in the extreme cases are the mere bogus coin of academic currency. ...

What are we to say, for example, to a course on *Clothing Analysis*, which the college curriculum says is 'designed to create in the student an enthusiasm for possessing individuality in clothes'? What an awakening of genius must this course occasion! One imagines some young inspired dreamer, waking in the night and leaping from his couch to seize a piece of chalk and sketch out an idea for the shape of his pants. Graduates returning to the farm with a gold medal for individuality in clothes would be pretty expensive to keep. Yet the course is given in a university with an honoured name and a hundred years of history. ...

In the same college is a department of Physical Education for women which has among other things a set of 'activities' courses. These include *Dry Skiing*, which ought to call for a balancing course in *Wet Golf*. In the list also appear 'life-saving,' a thing which, in my day, students left to the bartender at seven o'clock the next morning. But these people evidently have a good time all the time; they do tennis, sailing, archery, tap dancing and wind up with tumbling. It is only fair to add that various colleges list tap dancing and archery, and one has the hardihood to announce a course on the *Fundamentals of Golf for Beginners*. One can imagine the boy who is taking the

individual study in pants going out in plus fours to get his funda-
ment in golf. (TMC 138–9)

⁊

Everybody is aware of the vast amount of instruction that is carried
on to-day by correspondence courses. It is, I suppose literally true
that one may now acquire the whole of an education in this manner.
Not only is instruction given in all the various branches of learning,
but also in the practical arts. Courses are offered in telegraphy,
stenography, advertising, plumbing, and even in the purely mechanical things, such as short story writing, play writing, the making of
scenarios and how to earn a living by poetry.

   Everybody also has admired the clearness and simplicity with
which the manuals are composed. Take, for example, the one entitled, 'How to Learn the Alphabet by Correspondence.' The pictures
of the letters A, B and C are drawn with such absolute sincerity and
faith as to be unmistakable; while the pupil is gently led from C to
D, from D to E, until a knowledge of the whole alphabet is acquired
and the pupil is ready to pass on to volume 2, 'How to Synchronize
the Alphabet into Words.' (IM 186)

⁊

HOW TO COME IN OUT OF THE WET

A second section of the course, not to be attempted until section
one [HOW TO POUND SAND] has been thoroughly learned, gives practical instructions in How to Come in Out of the Wet. Like Section
I, it is illustrated with a little double illustration, the first part of
which is labelled, *He Didn't Come in*, and showing a young man
lying on his own doorstep on a rainy day – drowned. The other part
shows a young man, much better dressed, knocking at the door of a
house and saying, 'Let me in, mother, it's going to rain.' (IM 189)

⁊

They [written examinations] are the curse of education. They are also absolutely necessary. They spoil everything. And you can't do without them. Education without compulsory mechanical tests would, for the common run of us, turn to mush. If all I need for a degree in Persian literature is to go away and read it, or rather to come back and say I read it, I'll get it fast enough. That would do for a genius – that was the education of Isaac Newton and of Gibbon – but it is not for you. You've got to be examined as carefully as a horse. (HML 50)

But, in any case, examination tests are never the whole story. To those who know, a written examination is far from being a true criterion of capacity. It demands too much of mere memory, imitativeness, and the insidious willingness to absorb other people's ideas. Parrots and crows would do admirably in examinations. Indeed, the colleges are full of them. (MDE 89)

Leaving out the rotten schools and the snobbish schools, the decent boarding school has certain disciplines in life to offer, salutary and useful, not to be got elsewhere. One is the value of the break from home, of being compelled for the first time to stand on one's own feet. It is in choking down the sobs of homesickness that we first learn how much home has meant, and how fond we are of it, and the humbler and more dilapidated the home, the more suffocating is the sob of affection for it. (BLB 124)

We have long since discovered that we cannot know anything. Our studies consist only in the long-drawn proof of the futility for the search after knowledge effected by exposing the errors of the past. (ELS 27)

∾

We actually proceed on the silly supposition that you can 'examine'
a person in English literature, torture it out of him, so to speak, in
the course of a two hours' inquisition. We ask him to distinguish the
'styles' of different authors as he would the colour of their whiskers.
We expect him to divide up authors into 'schools' and to sort them
out as easily as a produce merchant classifies fish.

The truth is that you cannot examine in English in this way, or
only at the cost of killing the very thing that you wish to create. The
only kind of examination in the subject I can think of would be to
say to the pupil, for example, 'Have you read the novels of Charles
Dickens and do you like them?' and when he answered that he
didn't care for them but that his uncle read them all the time, to
send a B.A. degree to his uncle.

We make our pupils spend about two hours a day for ten years in
the silly pursuit of what we call English, and yet at the end of it we
wonder that our students have less real appreciation of literature in
them than when they read a half-dime novel for the sheer artistic joy
of it. (CoD 62–3)

∾

I regard courses in English literature as the very highest reach of our
studies in the humanities; to remove them, and rely upon a student's
spontaneous desire to read, would lead nowhere. It would but turn
the fresh springs of curiosity and interest to wander and perish in
the sands. (HML 58)

∾

The old classical education had at least the advantage that it was
hard and difficult with no royal road. It was as hard as ever a teacher
liked to make it. For witness call in anyone who has studied Greek
moods and tenses or tried to translate the Greek dramatists into
something intelligible. In all this it was miles above a great deal of

the slush and mush, which has in part replaced it, the effortless, pretentious studies of things that can't be studied at all, the vague fermentations that tend to replace stern disciplinary work when education is all paid for and free for all and popular and universal, provided that it is not made difficult. ... It always seems to me that in a lot of the revised education of today, which quite rightly undertook to modify the severities, the rigor, the physical punishment, and the needless difficulties of the older teaching, the mistake is made in the contrary direction. Everything is made too easy. The teacher has to 'sell' the subject to the class, and in trying to make everything clear and simple it is forgotten that there are some things that can't be made clear and simple because they are by nature difficult and complex. (BLB 145–7)

That was what gave him his literary taste. He used to read Ibsen and that other Dutch author – Bumstone Bumstone, isn't it? – and you can judge that he was a mighty intellectual fellow. He was so intellectual that he was, as he himself admitted, a complete eggnostic. He and Pupkin used to have the most tremendous arguments about creation and evolution, and how if you study at a school of applied science you learn that there's no hell beyond the present life. (SS 89)

These buildings [of the new university] are exceptionally fine, standing fifteen stories high and comparing favourably with the best departmental stores or factories in the City. Indeed, after nightfall, when they are all lighted up for the evening technical classes and when their testing machinery is in full swing and there are students going in and out in overall suits, people have often mistaken the university, or this newer part of it, for a factory. A foreign visitor once said that the students looked like plumbers, and President Boomer was so proud of it that he put the phrase into his next Commencement address; and from there the newspapers got it and the

Associated Press took it up and sent it all over the United States with the heading, 'Have Appearance of Plumbers; Plutoria University Congratulated on Character of Students,' and it was a proud day indeed for the heads of the Industrial Science faculty. ...

But the change both of name and of character from Concordia College to Plutoria University was the work of President Boomer. He had changed it from an old-fashioned college of the by-gone type to a university in the true modern sense. At Plutoria they now taught everything. Concordia College, for example, had no teaching of religion except lectures on the Bible. Now they had lectures also on Confucianism, Mohammedanism, Buddhism, with an optional course on atheism for students in the final year.

And, of course, they had long since admitted women, and there were now beautiful creatures with Cléo de Mérode hair studying astronomy at oaken desks and looking up at the teacher with eyes like comets. The university taught everything and did everything. It had whirling machines on the top of it that measured the speed of the wind, and deep in its basements it measured earthquakes with a seismograph; it held classes on forestry and dentistry and palmistry; it sent life classes into the slums, and death classes to the city morgue. It offered such a vast variety of themes, topics, and subjects to the students, that there was nothing that a student was compelled to learn, while from its own press in its own press-building it sent out a shower of bulletins and monographs like driven snow from a rotary plough. (AA 39–40)

'A splendid group of men, are they not?' said the president. 'We owe them much. This is the late Mr. Hogworth, a man of singularly large heart.' Here he pointed to a bronze figure wearing a wreath of laurel and inscribed GULIELMUS HOGWORTH, LITT.DOC. 'He had made a great fortune in the produce business, and wishing to mark his gratitude to the community, he erected the anemometer, the wind-measure, on the roof of the building, attaching to it no other condition than that his name should be printed in the weekly reports immediately beside the velocity of the wind. The figure beside him is the late Mr. Underbugg, who founded our lectures on the Four Gospels on the sole stipulation that henceforth any reference of ours to the four gospels should be coupled with his name.' (AA 42)

The whole professoriate was absorbed in one of those great educational crises which from time to time shake a university to its base. The meeting of the faculty that day bid fair to lose all vestige of decorum in the excitement of the moment. For, as Dean Elderberry Foible, the head of the faulty, said, the motion that they had before them amounted practically to a revolution. The proposal was nothing less than the permission of the use of lead-pencils instead of pen and ink in the sessional examinations of the university. Anyone conversant with the inner life of a college will realize that to many of the professoriate this was nothing less than a last wild onslaught of socialistic democracy against the solid bulwarks of society. They must fight it back or die on the walls. To others it was one more step in the splendid progress of democratic education, comparable only to such epoch-making things as the abandonment of the cap and gown, and the omission of the word 'sir' in speaking to a professor.

No wonder that the fight raged. Elderberry Foible, his fluffed white hair almost on end, beat in vain with his gavel for order. Finally, Chang of Physiology, who was a perfect dynamo of energy and was known frequently to work for three or four hours at a stretch, proposed that the faculty should adjourn the question and meet for its further discussion on the following Saturday morning. This revolutionary suggestion, involving work on Saturday, reduced the meeting to a mere turmoil, in the midst of which Elderberry Foible proposed that the whole question of the use of lead-pencils should be adjourned till that day six months, and that meantime a new special committee of seventeen professors, with power to add to their number, to call witnesses and, if need be, to hear them, should report on the entire matter *de novo*. This motion, after the striking out of the words *de novo* and the insertion of *ab initio*, was finally carried, after which the faculty sank back completely exhausted into its chair, the need of afternoon tea and toast stamped on every face. (AA 47–8)

In my own opinion, reached after fifty-two years of profound reflection, this system [of university education] contains in itself the seeds of destruction. It puts a premium on dullness and a penalty on genius. It circumscribes that latitude of mind which is the real spirit of learning. If we persist in it we shall presently find that true learning will fly away from our universities and will take rest wherever some individual and inquiring mind can mark out its path for itself. (MDE 82)

If I were founding a university – and I say it with all the seriousness of which I am capable – I would found first a smoking room; then when I had a little more money in hand I would found a dormitory; then after that, or more probably with it, a decent reading room and a library. After that, if I still had money over that I couldn't use, I would hire a professor and get some textbooks. (MDE 95)

It seems that recently [ca. 1926] there has been a lot of new trouble about the theory of evolution in the schools. ... A boy in a Kansas public school threw down his book and said that the next time he was called a protozoon he'd quit the class. A parent in Ostaboola, Oklahoma, wrote to the local school board to say that for anyone to teach his children that they were descended from monkeys cast a doubt upon himself which he found intolerable. (WW 7)

The comic college man [of the popular press] has a face cut square, like a strawberry box, a shoulder like a right angle, and a coat shaped like the forty-fifth proposition in Euclid. His face is drawn in a few lines, with the brains left out, and if he ever knew algebra, he gives no sign of it. In short, he is a nut.

When we see them, Nut No. 1, Gussie, is seated on the window-sill playing a ukulele, and Nut No. 2 has his ukulele ready to play as soon as Gussie runs out of ideas and jokes. The college man sleeps with his ukulele.

Gussie and Eddie have apparently the same passion for little dia-logue jokes as Tootsie and Maisie. These jokes, a generation ago [from ca. 1928], were put into the mouths of negroes and were called 'coon jokes'; or else they were divided up between 'Mike' and 'Pat' and called 'Irish humour'; but now they are known as 'college wit,' and every man at college cracks one every ten minutes. (SC 77)

My old students! There they were all over the West, in every town, – waiting for me, in some cases I was told, laying for me. But in any case they were there. Not so many graduates perhaps from the fac-ulty of Liberal Arts: Arts men find it harder to get work in the West now that there are so few livery stables. (MDW 264–5)

Speaking in a general way one may say that in the West McGill pre-dominates in medicine, Queen's in the Church and Toronto at (not behind) the Bar. Thus McGill attends the sick and when McGill medicine has done its work, Queen's buries them and when they're buried Toronto divides up their estates among the three. It is what Adam Smith so happily called the Division of Labour. (MDW 266)

In our economic life all is disunion – province against province and all against the Dominion, but we at least still have the bond of union represented by the common culture of our universities. (MDW 272)

Only I don't like the name – adult education. I wouldn't want any one to call me an 'adult.' That word never seems quite right; it always sounds like a halfwit. Don't they have homes for adults? No? Well, surely there are adults in some of the homes, and you can hang an adult, can't you? And of course, 'education' is a tainted word. It carries still its old false suggestion that it is something everybody had as a child, like measles, and doesn't need any longer. Say to any man, 'Look here, don't you think you need a little education, the kind they give to adults?' and see how he reacts to it. (RU 45)

Thus grew up that distinction between light and darkness, between God and the Devil, still seen in the separation of the Faculty of Arts from those of Medicine and Science. (HML 232)

Very few people can stand the strain of being educated without getting superior over it. (RU 57)

FAMILY

The family – the one institution in which the better side of human nature shines with an undimmed light. (UR 92)

But then what father ever would want to speak angrily to such a boy as Neil Pepperleigh? The judge took no credit himself for that; the finest grown boy in the whole county and so broad and big that they took him into the Missinaba Horse when he was only seventeen. And clever, – so clever that he didn't need to study; so clever that he used to come out at the foot of the class in mathematics at the Mariposa high school through sheer surplus of brain power. I've heard the judge explain it a dozen times. Why, Neil was so clever that he used to be able to play billiards at the Mariposa House all evening when the other boys had to stay at home and study. (SS 85–6)

The schoolmaster learns to know people as 'parents' and in this aspect, I say it without hesitation, they are all more or less insane. The parent's absorbing interest in his lop-eared boy (exactly like all other lop-eared boys), his conception of the importance of that slab-sided child and the place he occupies in the solar system, can only spring from an unbalanced mind. It is a useful delusion, I admit. Without it the world couldn't very well go on. The parent who could see his boy as he really is, would shake his head and say: 'Willie is no good; I'll sell him.' (ELS 186–7)

And, all the time, education grows longer and longer. This does not deny that the average human life is now longer. It means that paternity is shorter. People do not see enough of their grandchildren – the sweetest prospect in the world. Life has all too little evening. It has all run in arrears and never catches up. (TMC 5)

Homicide corresponds to general instinct in our nature and is bound to stay. The desire to kill people is quite natural. If I see a fiend in green goggles roar past me on a motor-cycle at a speed of fifty miles an hour, tearing my ears with noise, I want to kill him. Rightly so. It may be inexpedient to do it, but it would be the thing to do. I may want to kill an umpire, or a comedian or an after-dinner speaker – but to want to kill a whole nation, to poison and drown and destroy by machinery thousands of innocent beings, to pretend that little children are 'enemies,' and to want to starve them to death – ah! no, I won't do it. Don't ask me. War, in other words, has got on the wrong side of our parental feelings, and it's got to go. (DP 265–6)

FOOD AND DRINK

Eat what you want. Eat lots of it. Yes, eat too much of it. Eat till you can just stagger across the room with it and prop it up against a sofa cushion. Eat everything that you like until you can't eat any more. The only test is, can you pay for it? If you can't pay for it, don't eat it. And listen – don't worry as to whether your food contains starch, or albumen, or gluten, or nitrogen. If you are damn fool enough to want these things, go and buy them and eat all you want of them. Go to a laundry and get a bag of starch, and eat your fill of it. (LL 25)

Our medical people of today [ca. 1939] talk much of vitamins. Just what they are I do not know, but they are subdivided and named, with the rich imaginative fancy of the scientist, Vitamin A, Vitamin B, and so on as discovered. These I understand enter into our diet and have a peculiar importance in it. If we are misguided enough to stop eating any one of these vitamins, it is all over with us. When I first learned this, I was inclined, if only for precaution's sake, to give up bacon and eggs and roast beef and adopt an exclusive diet of vitamins as everywhere freely advertised at a price equal merely to what we have got. (TMC 47)

Mr. Rasselyer-Brown drank.

It was not meant that he was a drunkard or that he drank too much, or anything of that sort. He drank. That was all.

There was no excess about it. Mr. Rasselyer-Brown, of course, began the day with an eye-opener – and after all, what alert man does not wish his eyes well open in the morning? He followed it usually just before breakfast with a bracer – and what wiser precaution can a businessman take than to brace his breakfast? On his way to business he generally had his motor stopped at the Grand Palaver for a moment, if it was a raw day, and dropped in and took something to keep out the damp. If it was a cold day he took something to keep out the cold, and if it was one of those clear, sunny days that are so dangerous to the system he took whatever the bartender (a recognized health expert) suggested to tone the system up. After which he could sit down in his office and transact more business, and bigger business, in coal, charcoal, wood, pulp, pulpwood, and wood-pulp, in two hours than any other man in the business could in a week. Naturally so. For he was braced, and propped, and toned up, and his eyes had been opened, and his brain cleared, till outside of very big business, indeed, few men were on a footing with him. (AA 59–60)

I know nothing more dreadful at a dinner table than one of these amateur raconteurs – except perhaps, two of them. After about three stories have been told, there falls on the dinner table an uncomfortable silence, in which everybody is aware that everybody else is trying hard to think of another story, and is failing to find it. There is no peace in the gathering again till some man of firm and quiet mind turns to his neighbour and says, 'But after all there is no doubt that whether we like it or not prohibition is coming.' Then everybody in his heart says, 'Thank heaven!' and the whole tableful are happy and contented again, till one of the story-tellers 'thinks of another,' and breaks loose. (FF 162–3)

It [alcohol] gets, they tell me, into the brain. I don't dispute it. It turns the prosencephalon into mere punk. I know it. I've felt it doing it. They tell me – and I believe it – that after even one glass of alcohol, or shall we say Scotch whisky and soda, a man's working power is lowered by twenty per cent. This is a dreadful thing. After three glasses, so it is held, his capacity for sustained rigid thought is cut in two. And after about six glasses the man's working power is reduced by at least a hundred per cent. He merely sits there – in his arm-chair, at his club let us say – with all power, even all *desire* to work gone out of him, not thinking rigidly, not sustaining his thought, a mere shapeless chunk of geniality, half hidden in the blue smoke of his cigar. (FrF 110)

For the true aspect of the bounty of Nature, give me every time the sight of a butcher shop in autumn, with the pink lobsters nestling in the white celery, pure as snow. When the poet wanted inspiration he went and talked with a shepherd. I'd rather talk with a chef. (WW 84)

I am myself a believer in prohibition. I think that water, especially clear, cold water – I don't care for muddy water – is a beautiful drink. I had a glass of it the other day, and it seemed wonderfully limpid and transparent – almost like gin. (WWD 215)

But, of course, there's one good thing about not having to drink [under Prohibition], you certainly can eat. I mean, not only turkey and that but a lot of extra things. I ate celery all the time I was wait-ing for the turkey. You naturally do if there's no sherry. I ate bunches of it, and afterwards a lot of parsley and part of a table wreath by mistake. (RU 108)

HISTORY

For all wise thinking, for all careful social control, it is necessary to see things as they have grown, to look on our institutions in the light of their past. Such dim vision as we can have of the future depends absolutely on this. Cut off the human race from the knowledge and comprehension of its history, and its government will just turn into a monkey cage. We need the guidance of history. (TMC 50–1)

Historical rehabilitation is emphatically the order of the day, and it has become the peculiar province and the particular pride of the modern historian [ca. 1916] to expose the errors of his predecessors. His superior access to original sources of information enables him to direct upon the events of the past a flood of 'dry light' which reveals them in a new perspective. The lights and shadows are shifted upon the landscape of history. What formerly appeared imposing dwindles to the enlightened eye, and figures forgotten in the obscurity of ignorance are revealed in a new and majestic stature. The estimates of characters and achievement which have formed the commonplaces of our national knowledge are overthrown, and the temple of fame rudely cleared of its former inmates to make way for the smiling crowd of whitewashed sinners carrying each his new certificate of rehabilitation. (ELS 270–1)

Too much has been said of the heroes of history, – the strong men, the strenuous men, the troublesome men; too little of the amiable, the kindly, and the tolerant. It is perhaps the strenuous and the purposeful who keep the wheels of human progress moving, but it is the broad-minded tolerance of easy-going indolence that keeps the friction of opinion from clogging the machinery of progress. The strenuous men have had their apotheosis: their names are inscribed in brass, their busts are carved in stone on the temples and monuments of an admiring world. But where is the record of the nobly indolent, the names of those great men whose resolute inertia and whose self-denying negation of the necessity of effort have rendered possible the false eminence of their fellows? In the history of religious controversy the real progress has been made by those inspired with an intense lack of fixed opinion: the history of invention is the history of applied idleness. To shirk work is to abbreviate labour. To shirk argument is to settle controversy. To shirk war is to cherish peace. (ELS 273)

What I mean is this. We are in danger now, in our rushing mechanical world, of rearing a generation with no backward outlook, living in two dimensions only, without thought of the past. (TMC 50)

We [in Canada] can best learn to value this heritage of freedom by reflecting on its history. We can best appreciate the present in the light of the past, and in the same light we can realize the measure of our duty and obligation towards the future. (CFF xxiii)

Each of us in life is a prisoner. The past offers us, as it were a door of escape. We are set and bound in our confined lot. Outside, somewhere, is eternity; outside, somewhere, is infinity. We seek to reach into it and the pictured past seems to afford to us an outlet of escape. (HTT 281)

∽

Memory – the vivifying picture that our imagination conjures up of the Days that Were! Always better and greater than the days that are – that wistful feeling towards the past that each of us carries within him – the call, back through the years, to a lost identity. (MDW 272)

HUMOUR

Humour is the kindly contemplation of the incongruities of life, and the artistic expression thereof. (HH 15)

The essence of humour is human kindliness. (HH unpaginated preface)

Our sense of humour, like so much else about us, sprang from lowly and even discreditable origins. (HH 22)

In doing this [practice teaching] I learned on the side a lesson on how not to be funny, or the misuse of a sense of humour which lasted me all my life. ... The principal of the Strathroy Collegiate was Mr. James Wetherell, the well-beloved 'Jimmy' Wetherell whose memory is still dear to the heart of a thousand pupils. He seemed to us old at the time, as all adult people do to the eyes of eighteen, but he must have been relatively young, for he lived on and on, passed the opening century, still in harness when the Great War came, and died at a ripe age later on. He was a fine scholar, his chief subject, at least the one he liked best to teach, being English. But he had acquired, as most scholars do if absorbed in their work and exulting in the exposition of it, little tricks of speech and manner all his own and all too easy to imitate. I had at that time a certain natural gift of mimicry, could easily hit off people's voices and instinctively reproduce their gestures. So when Jimmy Wetherell, halfway through a lesson in English, said to me most courteously, 'Now will you take the lesson over at that point and continue it?' I did so with a completeness and resemblance to Jimmy's voice and manner which of course delighted the class. Titters ran through the room. Encouraged as an artist, I laid it on too thick. The kindly principal saw it himself and flushed pink. When I finished he said quietly, 'I am afraid I admire your brains more than your manners.' The words cut me to the quick. I felt them to be so true and yet so completely without malice. For I had no real 'nerve,' no real 'gall.' It was the art of imitation that appealed to me. I had not realized how it might affect the person concerned. I learned with it my first lesson in the need for human kindliness as an element in humour. (BLB 159–60)

Take puns. They have pretty well died out now. The last of the punsters is probably dead, or in hiding. But many of us can still remember the social nuisance of the inveterate punster. This man followed conversation as a shark follows a ship. (LaL 5)

I am quite sure that when Adam and Eve were put out of the Garden of Eden, Eve said, 'Well, thank goodness, Adam, we've got our sense of humour!' And Adam, trudging along deep in thought, paused and said, 'How's that?' – and took a first step towards getting one. 'I certainly had to laugh at that snake!' said Eve with a toss of her head and a false snigger. 'At the snake?' said Adam, and went on with his reflections.

  Years after Adam used to tell the whole story with the greatest humour. Eve didn't like his bringing it up. They had come up in the world since. (RU 99)

The Greek gods – their intelligence was very low – thought it funny

when Hephaestus (or somebody) fell out of Heaven and broke his
leg and walked with a limp. Heaven echoed with the laughter of the
gods. It must have been a hell of a heaven. (HTW 215)

In the first place, are witty people in general attractive to anybody?
Not as a rule. They get tiresome. It is terribly hard to be witty without getting conceited about it. I used to be very witty myself, till I
learned to be careful about it. People don't like it. There are two
things in ordinary conversation which ordinary people dislike –
information and wit. (LaL 3)

A peculiar interest always attaches to humour. There is no quality of
the human mind about which its possessor is more sensitive than the
sense of humour. A man will freely confess that he has no ear for
music, or no taste for fiction, or even no interest in religion. But I
have yet to see the man who announces that he has no sense of
humour. In point of fact, every man is apt to think himself possessed
of an exceptional gift in this direction, and that even if his humour
does not express itself in the power either to make a joke or to laugh
at one, it none the less consists in a peculiar insight or inner light
superior to that of other people. (MDE 170–1)

It is my candid opinion that no man ought to be allowed to tell a
funny story or anecdote without a licence. We insist rightly enough
that every taxi driver must have a licence, and the same principle
should apply to anybody who proposes to act as a *raconteur*. Telling a
story is a difficult thing – quite as difficult as driving a taxi. And the
risks of failure and accident and the unfortunate consequences of
such to the public, if not exactly identical, are, at any rate, analogous.
    This is a point of view not generally appreciated. A man is apt to

think that just because he has heard a good story he is able and entitled to repeat it. He might as well undertake to do a snake dance merely because he has seen Madame Pavlova do one. (MDE 186)

Burlesque writing at its best is a fine achievement. Nor need any writer be ashamed of it nor be misled into believing that he wastes his talents in devoting himself to it. If he has the peculiar talent he can find no better life work than that of a 'funny' writer. It is probable that such people, more than any other writers, have brought temporary solace to weary humanity, have coaxed laughter out of sorrow and brought to those distressed the respite of forgetfulness. If you are funny, keep funny even if it makes you sad. (HTW 240)

The new indifference called religious tolerance was spreading rapidly [in the eighteenth century]. Without this broad and kindly outlook humour is not possible. (HTT 251)

The final stage of the development of humour is reached when amusement no longer arises from a single 'funny' idea, meaningless contrast, or odd play upon words, but rests upon a prolonged and sustained conception of the incongruities of human life itself. The shortcomings of our existence, the sad contrast of our aims and our achievements, the little fretting aspiration of the day that fades into the nothingness of to-morrow, kindle in the mellowed mind a sense of gentle amusement from which all selfish exultation has been chastened by the realization of our common lot of sorrow. On this higher plane humour and pathos mingle and become one. To the Creator perhaps in retrospect the little story of man's creation and his fall seems sadly droll. (ELS 92–3)

Humour in its highest reach mingles with pathos: it voices sorrow for our human lot and reconciliation with it. (HH 232)

∞

It is difficult to be funny and great at the same time. Aristophanes and Molière and Mark Twain must sit below Aristotle and Bossuet and Emerson. (CD 306)

∞

All Dickens's humour couldn't save Dickens, save him from his overcrowded life, its sordid and neurotic central tragedy and its premature collapse. But Dickens's humour, and all such humour, has saved or at least greatly served the world. (RU 91)

∞

Just as the parasite may bring to the parent-plant elements of life and sustenance and purify it from disease, so the parasitic forms of literature may serve to invigorate and purify the whole body of letters. (HTT 46–7)

∞

The basis of the humorous, the amusing, the ludicrous, lies in the incongruity, the unfittingness, the want of harmony among things. (ELS 86)

∞

Laughter is the last refuge of sorrow or oppression. (RU 97)

∞

Humour is essentially a comforter, reconciling us to things as they are in contrast to things as they might be. (GF ix)

∞

Satire may be of a dozen kinds and used for a dozen purposes. It may be personal, malicious, diabolical, or political and colourless, just a stick to beat a dog. But humour is the very life of it. (HH 188)

⨏

The humour of willful imbecility lives forever. (RU 52)

⨏

Humour in a world of waning beliefs remains like Hope still left at the bottom of Pandora's box when all the evils of the Gods flew out from it upon the world. (HTT 15)

⨏

The kind of humour that is here described seems to me to reflect the humour of the highest culture, the humour of the future. Its distinction is its kindliness. It does not belong to the literature of effort, of strong convictions and animating purpose. It is rather that of disillusionment, of loss of faith, and the wide charity of mind that has come with the shattering of narrower ideals, not yet replaced. (HTT 205–6)

⨏

[Discussions of humour are] left to writers on philosophy and psychology, and it is amazing how dull scientific people can be when they try. (HH 12)

⨏

A humorous person, I think, would be apt to be cut more nearly to the heart by unkindness, more deeply depressed by adversity, more elated by sudden good fortune, than a person with but little of that quick sense of contrast and incongruity which is the focus of the humorous point of view. (RU 92)

⨏

Let me hear the comedian's own laughter come first and mine shall follow readily enough, laughing not *at* him but *with* him. I admit that when the comedian adopts this mode he runs the terrible risk of being the only one to laugh at his own fun. This is indeed dreadful. There is no contempt so bitter as that of the man who will not laugh for the man who will. (GF viii)

❧

The highest humour ... represents an outlook upon life, a retrospect as it were, in which is contrasted the fever and fret of our earthly lot with its shortcomings, its lost illusions and its inevitable end. (HTT 280)

❧

Humour is saved from [indifference, cruelty, and self-indulgence] by having made first acquaintance and then union with pathos, meaning here, pity for human suffering. (HH 232–3)

❧

Civilization's best legacy, thus far, is the world's humour. (RU 91)

❧

Exactly the converse to the Face Value form is found when words and phrases are rushed forward into a significance which they won't bear on closer inspection ... The author of the present work ... has probably made more extended use of this than any other person who has written as copiously. (HTT 39)

❧

I do not think that there is any doubt that educated people possess a far wider range of humour than the uneducated class. Some people, of course, get overeducated and become hopelessly academic. The word 'highbrow' has been invented exactly to fit the case. The sense of humour in the highbrow has become atrophied, or, to vary the metaphor, it is submerged or buried under the accumulated strata of

his education, on the top soil of which flourishes a fine growth of
conceit. But even in the highbrow the educated appreciation of
humour is there – way down. Generally, if one attempts to amuse a
highbrow he will resent it as if the process were beneath him; or perhaps the intellectual jealousy and touchiness with which he is always
overcharged will lead him to retaliate with a pointless story from
Plato. (MDE 179–80)

∽

And yet, after all, it seems that the world likes a little bit of kindliness, the 'touch of nature that makes the whole world kin'; and
likes, by force of association, the person or the thing with which the
kindliness is connected. Indeed, if a 'sense of humour' means, as it
should, something genial and kindly, something 'human' in the best
and largest sense, then perhaps it is, after all, one of the best 'business assets' that a man can have.

In other words, the beginning part of this essay is all wrong.
(SC 89)

LOVE

You cannot depict love inside a frame of fact. It needs a mist to dissolve in. You cannot tell a love story just as it is – because it isn't. There is something else there, something higher than our common selves and perhaps truer. When a young man sees in his girl an angel, and a young girl sees in her lover a hero, perhaps they are seeing what is really there – the self we each might have but which we grasp only in our higher moments and too late. (HTW 106)

All lovers – silly lovers in their silly stage – attain for a moment this super-self, each as towards the other. Each sees in the other what would be there for all the world to see in each of us, if we could but reach it ... till the light passes and is gone. 'All the world loves a lover' – of course; one can see easily why. (RU 122)

Isolde would wander forth from the castle at earliest morn, with the name of Guido on her lips. She told his name to the trees. She whispered it to the flowers. She breathed it to the birds. Quite a lot of them knew it. At times she would ride her palfrey along the sands of the sea and call 'Guido' to the waves! At other times she would tell it to the grass or even to a stick of cordwood or a ton of coal. (NN 44–5)

For the Little Girl in Green looked at Mr. Spillikins with wide eyes, and when she looked at him she saw all at once such wonderful things about him as nobody had ever seen before.

For she could see from the poise of his head how awfully clever he was; and from the way he stood with his hands in his side pockets she could see how manly and brave he must be; and of course there was firmness and strength written all over him. In short, she saw as she looked such a Peter Spillikins as truly never existed, or could exist – or at least such a Peter Spillikins as no one else in the world had ever suspected before. (AA 90–1)

The three were always together. At times, at the theatre, Dorothea and Vere would sit downstairs and Mr. Overgold in the gallery; at other times, Vere and Mr. Overgold would sit in the gallery and Dorothea downstairs; at times, one of them would sit in Row A, another in Row B, and a third in Row C; at other times, two would sit in Row B and one in Row C; at the opera, at times, one of the three would sit listening, the others talking, at other times, two listening and one talking, and, at other times, three talking and none listening.

Thus the three formed together one of the most perplexing, maddening triangles that ever disturbed the society of the metropolis. (MLL 20–1)

He first saw her – by one of the strangest coincidences in the world – on the Main Street of Mariposa. If he hadn't happened to be going up the street and she to be coming down it, the thing wouldn't have happened. Afterwards they both admitted that it was one of the most peculiar coincidences they ever heard of. Pupkin owned that he had had the strangest feeling that morning as if something were going to happen – a feeling not at all to be classed with the one of which he had once spoken to Miss Lawson, and which was, at the most a mere anticipation of respect.

But, as I say, Pupkin met Zena Pepperleigh on the 26th of June, at twenty-five minutes to eleven. And at once the whole world changed. The past was all blotted out. Even in the new forty volume edition of the 'Instalment Record of Humanity' that Mallory Tompkins had just received – Pupkin wouldn't have bothered with it.

She – that word henceforth meant Zena – had just come back from her boarding-school, and of all times of year for coming back from a boarding-school and for wearing a white shirt waist and a crimson tie and for carrying a tennis racket on the stricken street of a town – commend me to the month of June in Mariposa.

And, for Pupkin, straight away the whole town was irradiated with sunshine, and there was such a singing of the birds, and such a dancing of the rippled waters of the lake, and such a kindliness in the faces of all the people, that only those who have lived in Mariposa, and been young there, can know at all what he felt.

The simple fact is that just the moment he saw Zena Pepperleigh, Mr. Pupkin was clean, plumb, straight, flat, absolutely in love with her.

Which fact is so important that it would be folly not to close the chapter and think about it. (SS 91–2)

LUCK

A man called me the other day with the idea of insuring my life. Now, I detest life-insurance agents; they always argue that I shall some day die, which is not so. I have been insured a great many times, for about a month at a time, but have had no luck with it at all. (LL 90)

To think of all these people so eager and anxious to catch the steamer, and some of them running to catch it, and so fearful that they might miss it, – the morning of a steamboat accident. And the captain blowing his whistle, and warning them so severely that he would leave them behind, – leave them out of the accident! And everybody crowding so eagerly to be in the accident.

Perhaps life is like that all through. (SS 39)

I am a great believer in luck, and I find the harder I work the more of it I have. (Attributed)

MARIPOSA

In regard to the present work [*Sunshine Sketches of a Little Town*] I must disclaim at once all intentions of trying to do anything so ridiculously easy as writing about a real place and real people. Mariposa is not a real town. On the contrary, it is about seventy or eighty of them. You may find them all the way from Lake Superior to the sea, with the same square streets and the same maple trees and the same churches and hotels, and everywhere the sunshine of the land of hope. ...

The inspiration of the book, – a land of hope and sunshine where little towns spread their square streets and their trim maple trees beside placid lakes almost within echo of the primeval forest, – is large enough. If it fails in its portrayal of the scenes and the country that it depicts the fault lies rather with an art that is deficient than in an affection that is wanting. (SS xvii–xviii)

This was Mr. Golgotha Gingham, the undertaker of Mariposa, and his dress was due to the fact that he had just come from what he called an 'interment.' Mr. Gingham had the true spirit of his profession, and such words as 'funeral' or 'coffin' or 'hearse' never passed his lips. He spoke always of 'interments,' of 'caskets,' and 'coaches,' using terms that were calculated rather to bring out the majesty and sublimity of death than to parade its horrors.

To be present at the hotel was in accord with Mr. Gingham's general conception of his business. No man had ever grasped the true principles of undertaking more thoroughly than Mr. Gingham. I have often heard him explain that to associate with the living, uninteresting though they appear, is the only way to secure the custom of the dead.

'Get to know people really well while they are alive,' said Mr. Gingham; 'be friends with them, close friends, and then when they die you don't need to worry. You'll get the order every time.' (SS 9)

Up in front of the little deck forward of the pilot house was a group of the older men, Mullins and Duff and Mr. Smith in a deck chair, and beside him Mr. Golgotha Gingham, the undertaker of Mariposa, on a stool. It was part of Mr. Gingham's principles to take in an outing of this sort, a business matter, more or less, – for you never know what may happen at these water parties. At any rate, he was there in a neat suit of black, not, of course, his heavier or professional suit, but a soft clinging effect as of burnt paper that combined gaiety and decorum to a nicety. (SS 42)

Everybody knew Jeff and liked him, but the odd thing was that till he made money nobody took any stock in his ideas at all. It was only after he made the 'clean up' that they came to see what a splendid fellow he was. 'Level-headed' I think was the term; indeed in the speech of Mariposa, the highest form of endowment was to have the head set on horizontally as with a theodolite. (SS 19–20)

You see, in Mariposa, shaving isn't the hurried, perfunctory thing that it is in the city. A shave is looked upon as a form of physical pleasure and lasts anywhere from twenty-five minutes to three-quarters of an hour. (SS 23)

❧

Did I mention Myra, Jeff's daughter? Perhaps not. That's the trouble with the people in Mariposa; they're all so separate and so different – not a bit like the people in the cities – that unless you hear about them separately and one by one you can't for a moment understand what they're like. (SS 28)

❧

I thought that perhaps getting so much money, – well, you know the way it acts on people in the larger cities. It seemed to spoil one's idea of Jeff that copper and asbestos and banana lands should form the goal of his thought when, if he knew it, the little shop and the sunlight of Mariposa was so much better. (SS 31)

❧

Half-past six on a July morning! The Mariposa Belle is at the wharf, decked in flags, with steam up ready to start.

Excursion day!

Half-past six on a July morning, and Lake Wissanotti lying in the sun as calm as glass. The opal colours of the morning light are shot from the surface of the water.

Out on the lake the last thin threads of the mist are clearing away like flecks of cotton wool.

The long call of the loon echoes over the lake. The air is cool and fresh. There is in it all the new life of the land of the silent pine and the moving waters. Lake Wissanotti in the morning sunlight! Don't talk to me of the Italian lakes, or the Tyrol or the Swiss Alps. Take them away. Move them somewhere else. I don't want them. (SS 35)

❧

In Mariposa practically everybody belongs to the Knights of Pythias just as they do to everything else. That's the great thing about the town and that's what makes it so different from the city. Everybody is in everything. (SS 36)

I suppose that all excursions when they start are much the same. Anyway, on the Mariposa Belle everybody went running up and down all over the boat with deck chairs and camp stools and baskets, and found places, splendid places to sit, and then got scared that there might be better ones and chased off again. People hunted for places out of the sun and when they got them swore that they weren't going to freeze to please anybody; and the people in the sun said that they hadn't paid fifty cents to be roasted. Others said that they hadn't paid fifty cents to get covered with cinders, and there were still others who hadn't paid fifty cents to get shaken to death with the propeller.

Still, it was all right presently. The people seemed to get sorted out into the places on the boat where they belonged. The women, the older ones, all gravitated into the cabin on the lower deck and by getting round the table with needlework, and with all the windows shut, they soon had it, as they said themselves, just like being at home. (SS 41)

Everybody in Mariposa remembers the building of the church. First of all they had demolished the little stone church to make way for the newer Evidence. It seemed almost a sacrilege, as the Dean himself said, to lay hands on it. Indeed it was at first proposed to take the stone of it and build it into a Sunday School, as a lesser testimony. Then, when that proved impracticable, it was suggested that the stone be reverently fashioned into a wall that should stand as a token. And when even that could not be managed, the stone of the little church was laid reverently into a stone pile; afterwards it was devoutly sold to a building contractor, and, like so much else in life, was forgotten. (SS 58)

I don't think that at first anybody troubled much about the debt on

the church. Dean Drone's figures showed that it was only a matter of
time before it would be extinguished; only a little effort was needed,
a little girding up of the loins of the congregation and they could
shoulder the whole debt and trample it under their feet. Let them
but set their hands to the plough and they could soon guide it into
the deep water. Then they might furl their sails and sit every man
under his own olive tree. (SS 60)

∾

Then Mullins read a letter from the Mayor of Mariposa – Pete
Glover was mayor that year – stating that his keenest desires were
with them: and then one from the Carriage Company saying that its
heartiest good will was all theirs; and then one from the Meat Works
saying that its nearest thoughts were next to them. Then he read one
from himself, as head of the Exchange Bank, you understand,
informing him that he had heard of his project and assuring him of
his liveliest interest in what he proposed. (SS 70)

∾

Because, mind you, the Mariposa girls are all right. You've only to
look at them to realize that. You see, you can get in Mariposa a print
dress of pale blue or pale pink for a dollar twenty that looks infinitely better than anything you ever see in the city, – especially if
you can wear with it a broad straw hat and a background of maple
trees and the green grass of a tennis court. And if you remember,
too, that these are cultivated girls who have all been to the Mariposa
high school and can do decimal fractions, you will understand that
an Algerian corsair would sharpen his scimitar at the very sight of
them.

Don't think either that they are all dying to get married; because
they are not. I don't say they wouldn't take an errant knight, or a
buccaneer or a Hungarian refugee, but for the ordinary marriages of
ordinary people they feel nothing but a pitying disdain. So it is that
each one of them in due time marries an enchanted prince and goes

to live in one of the little enchanted houses in the lower part of the town.

I don't know whether you know it, but you can rent an enchanted house in Mariposa for eight dollars a month, and some of the most completely enchanted are the cheapest. As for the enchanted princes, they find them in the strangest places, where you never expected to see them, working – under a spell, you understand, – in drug-stores and printing offices, and even selling things in shops. But to be able to find them you have first to read ever so many novels about Sir Galahad and the Errant Quest and that sort of thing. (SS 94)

Let me begin at the beginning. Everybody in Mariposa is either a Liberal or a Conservative or else is both. Some of the people are or have been Liberals or Conservatives all their lives and are called dyed-in-the-wool Grits or old-time Tories and things of that sort. These people get from long training such a swift penetrating insight into national issues that they can decide the most complicated question in four seconds: in fact, just as soon as they grab the city papers out of the morning mail, they know the whole solution of any problem you can put to them. There are other people whose aim it is to be broad-minded and judicious and who vote Liberal or Conservative according to their judgment of the questions of the day. If their judgment of these questions tells them that there is something in it for them in voting Liberal, they do so. But if not, they refuse to be the slaves of a party or the henchmen of any political leader. So that anybody looking for henches has got to keep away from them. (SS 118–19)

Let me begin at the beginning. Everybody in Mariposa is either a Liberal or a Conservative or else is both. Some of the people are or have been Liberals or Conservatives all their lives and are called

The king, of course, is very well known, very favourably known, in Mariposa. Everybody remembers how he visited the town on his great tour in Canada, and stopped off at the Mariposa station.

Although he was only a prince at the time, there was quite a big crowd down at the depôt and everybody felt what a shame it was that the prince had no time to see more of Mariposa, because he would get such a false idea of it, seeing only the station and the lumber yards. Still, they all came to the station and all the Liberals and Conservatives mixed together perfectly freely and stood side by side without any distinction, so that the prince should not observe any party differences among them. And he didn't, – you could see that he didn't. They read him an address all about the tranquillity and loyalty of the Empire, and they purposely left out any reference to the trouble over the town wharf or the big row there had been about the location of the new post-office. There was a general decent feeling that it wouldn't be fair to disturb the prince with these things: later on, as king, he would, of course, *have* to know all about them, but meanwhile it was better to leave him with the idea that his empire was tranquil.

So they deliberately couched the address in terms that were just as reassuring as possible and the prince was simply delighted with it. I am certain that he slept pretty soundly after hearing that address. Why, you could see it taking effect even on his aides-de-camp and the people round him, so imagine how the prince must have felt! (SS 120–1)

Election times are exciting enough even in the city. But there the excitement dies down in business hours. In Mariposa there aren't any business hours and the excitement goes on *all* the time. (SS 128)

But of course 'home' would hardly be the word you would apply to the little town, unless perhaps, late at night, when you'd been sitting reading in a quiet corner somewhere such a book as the present one. (SS 141)

∽

As you sit back half dreaming in the car, you keep wondering why it is that you never came up before in all these years. Ever so many times you planned that just as soon as the rush and strain of business eased up a little, you would take the train and go back to the little town to see what it was like now, and if things had changed much since your day. But each time when your holidays came, somehow you changed your mind and went down to Naragansett or Naga-huckett or Nagasomething, and left over the visit to Mariposa for another time. (SS 143–4)

∽

What? it feels nervous and strange to be coming here again after all these years? It must indeed. No, don't bother to look at the reflection of your face in the window-pane shadowed by the night outside. Nobody could tell you now after all these years. Your face has changed in these long years of money-getting in the city. Perhaps if you had come back now and again, just at odd times, it wouldn't have been so. (SS 145)

∽

You may talk as you will about the intoning choirs of your European cathedrals, but the sounds of 'O-Can-a-da,' borne across the waters of a silent lake at evening is good enough for those of us who know Mariposa.

I think that it was just as they were singing like this: 'O – Can-a-da,' that word went round that the boat was sinking. (SS 46)

MODERN LIFE

There are many younger people now, so we are told, who do not read Dickens. Nor is it to be wondered at. We live in a badly damaged world [ca. 1933]. It is a world of flickering shadows, tossed by electric currents, of a babel of voices on the harassed air, a world of inconceivable rapidity, of instantaneous effects, of sudden laughter and momentary tragedy, where every sensation is made and electrocuted in a second and passes into oblivion. It is a world in which nothing lives. Art itself is as old as man, and as immortal. But the form and fashion of it change. Dickens lived and wrote in a world that is visibly passing. (CD 2)

ALL IS NOT GOLD THAT GLITTERS

How perfectly ridiculous! Everybody in the days in which we live [ca. 1926] knows – even a child knows – that all *is* gold that glitters. Put on clothes enough, appearance enough and you will be accepted anywhere. Just do a little glittering and everybody will think you are gold. Make a show, be a humbug, and you will succeed so fast that presently, being very wealthy and prominent, you will really think yourself a person of great merit and intellect. In other words, the glitter makes the gold. That is all there *is* to it. Gold is really one of the most useless of all material objects. Even now we have found no *real* use for it, except to fill our teeth. Any other employment of it is just *glitter*. So the proverb might be revised to read:

Every thing or person may be said to stand in high esteem and to pass at a high value provided that it or he makes a sufficient show, glitter, or appearance, the estimation being in inverse relation to the true quantitative measurement of the reality of it, them or her. That makes a neat workable proverb, expressed with up-to-date accuracy. (WW 60)

∽

VALPARAISO, Chile, June 1, 1932. – Two high school girls from the Tacoma (Wash.) Academy swam in here by mistake. They were heading for London via Panama, but missed the entry to the canal in a mist. They report things quiet on the west coast of South America, but passed a school of school teachers swimming from Callao to Vancouver.

HAMBURG, June 15, 1933. – Hans Hamfat of Hamburg completed to-day the first ocean swim attempted as a freight-carrier. Hamfat, who weighs three hundred and fifty pounds, carried nearly half a ton of mixed cargo across from Norway at a rate that cut far below the ordinary freight charges. It is proposed to incorporate him and let him swim back and forward to America.

In other words, by that time this hurried and hustling world [ca. 1928] will have overdone and done to death the swimming business, as it does everything else. It will go the way of the 1897 bicycle and the 1912 tango and all the other hobbies of a restless generation.

Why can't we take things a little quietly? (SC 123–4)

∽

And in the whole of Edward Aspiration Smith's career the only part I can take will be to bet on him in each successive contest that he carries on. That is exactly where we are getting to, those of us who are not world people ourselves – the excluded two billion who don't weigh 420 pounds, and can't jump eight feet in the air, who can't sing to 10,000 people, or pound anybody to a pulp in the presence of 120,000 others. We just bet. That's us and that's all that we amount to.

To-day, for example, there is a World's Horse running in a World Race in Cuba. I'm betting on that. And there's a World Man swimming the Irish Channel – or, no, he's drowned; but, anyway, there's some man swimming some channel somewhere – a World Channel – he's doing it for a World Belt or something. Anyway, I am betting on him. Why wouldn't I? Personally, I couldn't swim across the Lachine Canal. So all I can do is bet. You too. (SC 128–9)

⚬⚬⚬

The moving picture, so far [ca. 1939], has not sinned beyond the legitimate exaggeration of romantic art. What it will do next, we don't know, except that it will give the people what the people want. If they tire of accuracy and want Charlemagne to be a little more comic and wear a tuxedo; or if, as is likely, they presently want the epochs mixed up, so as to have Abraham Lincoln and Julius Caesar in the same film, they'll get that also. (TMC 40)

⚬⚬⚬

And now [ca. 1942] I will say one further thing about the classics. *There are not going to be any more.* We have them all now, all that there are ever going to be.

I cannot imagine any judgment more likely to meet with instant dissent, and to be dismissed with contempt or laughter. It sounds like the opinion of an aging man, for whom the world is running out with his own years. Such judgments are familiar. But I don't think that this is one. As I see it, the pre-eminence of written books reached its height in the nineteenth century, when for the first time all the world went to school and before all the world went to moving pictures and listened in on the radio. ...

So my prophecy of a classicless age to come is a safe one. By the time it's due, it won't matter. 'You said at the last election,' complained once an old farmer to me, 'that the price of marsh hay would go up.' 'Yes,' I answered, 'but the election's over.' So let it be with the withering grass of literature. (RU 60–1)

∽

The motor car did that. It did it all. The only amusement for a youth came to be going out in a car with a girl, or going out in a car to look for a girl, or going out with a girl to look for a car. Since you can't drive all the time, they had to invent the pop and hot dog stand, and since you can't stand and eat all evening, they had to build a dance hall beside the pop stand.

You can't dance forever, so that had to expand into a sort of Inn, called the Old Saw Mill, or the Old Forge, or the old anything at all that a new thing isn't.

With that, money, money, money every minute ... money for gasoline, money for pop, money for ice cream, more money for more gas, money for the right to dance, money for the right not to dance ... (LaL 30)

∽

A book is said to be *arresting, gripping, compelling*. It has got to hold the reader down so that he can't get up. A preacher has got to be *vital, dynamic*; he must *put his sermon over*; he must pitch it at the audience; in short, preaching becomes a form of baseball with the clergyman in the box.

In other words the whole of our life and thought has got to be restated in terms of moving things, in terms of electricity, radio and all the crackling physical apparatus of the world in which we live [ca. 1926]. (WW 46)

NONSENSE

The landlady of a boarding-house is a parallelogram – that is, an oblong angular figure, which cannot be described, but which is equal to anything. (LL 11)

A little beyond the City and further down the river the visitor finds this district of London terminating in the gloomy and forbidding Tower, the principal penitentiary of the city. Here Queen Victoria was imprisoned for many years. (MDE 41)

You know, many a man realises late in life that if when he was a boy he had known what he knows now, instead of being what he is he might be what he won't; but how few boys stop to think that if they knew what they don't know instead of being what they will be, they wouldn't be? These are awful thoughts. (LL 19)

'The limpid waters of Lake Owatawetness (the name, according to the old Indian legends of the place, signifies, The Mirror of the Almighty) abound with every known variety of fish. Near to its surface, so close that the angler may reach out his hand and stroke them, schools of pike, pickerel, mackerel, doggerel, and chickerel jostle one another in the water. They rise instantaneously to the bait and swim gratefully ashore holding it in their mouths. In the middle depth of the waters of the lake, the sardine, the lobster, the kippered herring, the anchovy and other tinned varieties of fish disport themselves with evident gratification, while even lower in the pellucid depths the dog-fish, the hog-fish, the log-fish, and the sword-fish whirl about in never-ending circles.

'Nor is Lake Owatawetness merely an Angler's Paradise. Vast forests of primeval pine slope to the very shores of the lake, to which descend great droves of bears – brown, green, and bear coloured – while as the shades of evening fall, the air is loud with the lowing of moose, cariboo, antelope, cantelope, musk-oxes, musk-rats, and other graminivorous mammalia of the forest. These enormous quadrumana generally move off about 10:30 p.m., from which hour until 11:45 p.m. the whole shore is reserved for bison and buffalo.

'After midnight hunters who so desire it can be chased through the woods, for any distance and at any speed they select, by jaguars, panthers, cougars, tigers, and jackals whose ferocity is reputed to be such that they will tear the breeches off a man with their teeth in their eagerness to sink their fangs in his palpitating flesh. Hunters, attention! Do not miss such attractions as these!' (LL 122–3)

∞

The horse is entirely covered with hair; the bicycle is not entirely covered with hair, except the '89 model they are using in Idaho ... There are no handles to a horse, but the 1910 model has a string to each side off its face for turning its head when there is anything you want it to see. (LL 125–6)

∞

She got up earlier and earlier. She now rose yesterday afternoon. (LL 136)

∞

COLLEGE PUBLIC LECTURE ON EDWARD GIBBON
As Reported by a Gibbon Ape
The Chairman called the audience together with a couple of short

barks after which he gave a series of whines to express his dis-approval of the lateness of the audience in coming in. He then introduced the lecturer by rubbing his hands together as a sign of pleasure, giving a series of not unfriendly growls in his direction. The lecturer then stood up and rubbed his hands together towards the audience as a sign of good will, opened his lecture with a couple of short yelps which elicited corresponding yelps from the audience. After that he settled down for half an hour to a steady series of grunts which seemed to soothe the listeners. But after this first period the lecturer began to bark, to move up and down, but not threateningly, on the platform, while at times he gurgled in such a friendly manner that a great number of the audience gurgled with him. At times also he heightened the effect of the gurgle by an appealing whine, and closed the lecture with a prolonged howl fol-lowed by a final heavy bark. The audience broke into loud yelps and clapped their hands. The chairman then invited another man to give a few satisfied grunts as an expression of thanks – and the meeting broke up, all barking. (HTW 184–5)

The scene is all so quiet and still and unbroken, that Miss Cleghorn, – the sallow girl in the telephone exchange, that I spoke of – said she'd like to be buried there. But all the people were so busy getting their baskets and gathering up their things that no one had time to attend to it. (SS 45)

The extraordinary advantage of *Balso* lies in the wide range of its use. In the first place, it undoubtedly heals all forms of bone disease when rubbed on the bones. For all internal complaints – especially those indicated by a sinking or depressed feeling, or a forlorn sensa-tion, or by an inability to earn money – *Balso* effects an immediate cure. In these cases it is taken internally, by the pint. For diseases of the hair, such as complete baldness or lethargy of the scalp, a smart rubbing of *Balso* will work wonders; while for infantile complaints, such as croup, whoop, paresis, and so forth, the child should be rubbed with *Balso* and laid upon a shelf. (GF 92)

❧

Suicide is a thing that ought not to be committed without very careful thought. It often involves serious consequences, and in some cases brings pain to others than oneself.

I don't say that there is no justification for it. There often is. Anybody who has listened to certain kinds of music, or read certain kinds of poetry, or heard certain kinds of performances upon the concertina, will admit that there are some lives which ought not to be continued, and that even suicide has its brighter aspects. (SS 104)

❧

'What a wonderful picture!' she murmured half to herself, half aloud, and half not aloud and half not to herself. (MLL 14)

❧

We are all descended from monkeys. This descent, however, took place a long time ago and there is no shame in it now. It happened two or three thousand years ago and must have been after and not before the Trojan war. (WW 8)

❧

The same kind of change passed over all the animals. All the animals are descended from one another. The horse is really a bird, and is the same animal as the crow. The differences between them are purely superficial. If a crow had two more feet and no feathers it would be a horse except for its size.

The whole of these changes were brought about by what is called the Survival of the Fittest. The crookedest snake outlived the others. Each creature had to adapt itself or bust.

The giraffe lengthened its neck. The stork went in for long legs. The hedgehog developed prickles. The skunk struck out an independent line of its own. Hence the animals that we see about us – as the skunk, the toad, the octopus, and the canary – are a highly selected lot. (WW 8)

༄

[From Darwin's diary] 'On the Antilles the common crow, or decapod, has two feet while in the Galapagos Islands it has a third. This third foot, however, does not appear to be used for locomotion, but merely for conversation.' (WW 9)

༄

It has recently been calculated by Professor Crook (graduate of Harvard and Sing Sing) that within forty years [of ca. 1926] every other man will belong to the criminal class; and even the man who isn't the other man will be pretty tough himself. (WW 114)

༄

And I have wondered, too, whether something might not be done to apply this wonderful and happy system of transformations [as used in the movies ca. 1928] to some of the old masterpieces of the stage and literature. They are too sad. The tragedy is all right and very interesting, but it ought to be redeemed at the end by putting in a quarter-second of first-class movie work.

Take, for example, Hamlet. All the world knows how the sorrow accumulates. Hamlet's father murdered, even before the play begins; his mother married to his uncle; Polonius stabbed; Ophelia drowned; Hamlet himself half crazy; his uncle killed; Yorick's skull mislaid; Laertes about to kill Hamlet – in short, a quite serious situation.

But that wonderful quarter-second of the movies would straighten it all out. Try this, for example:

YET EVEN HERE LOVE SNATCHES THIS WAYWARD SOUL FROM FATE –

And what do you see? Hamlet sitting beside Ophelia – she was not drowned, only got muddy and since has had time to wash – in the gardens of the Palace; and in another moment we find, smiling at them, his uncle, the King, no longer wicked; in fact he says himself:

WE DIDN'T UNDERSTAND ONE ANOTHER, HAM,

and near them playing on the grass, the inevitable child, only this time it is Hamlet's and Ophelia's. (SC 107–8)

THE STORY OF ADAM AND EVE
Technical Report on Its Adaptation for the Film

'We have looked over this MS. with reference to the question of adapting it to a scenario. We find the two principal characters finely and boldly drawn and both well up to the standard of the moving picture. The man Adam – Christian name only given in the MS. – appeals to us very strongly as a primitive but lovable nature. Adam has "pep" and we think that we could give him an act among the animals, involving the very best class of menagerie and trapeze work which would go over big.

'But we consider that Adam himself would get over better if he represented a more educated type and we wish therefore to make Adam a college man, preferably from a western university.

'We think similarly that the principal female character, Eve, would appeal more directly to the public if it was made clear that she was an independent woman with an avocation of her own. We propose to make her a college teacher of the out-of-door woodland dances now [ca. 1928] so popular in the leading women's universities.

'It is better that Adam and Eve should not be married at the opening of the scenario but at the end after they have first found themselves and then found one another.

'We find the "Garden" lonely and the lack of subordinate characters mystifying; we also find the multiplicity of animals difficult to explain without a special setting.

'We therefore propose to remove the scene to the Panama Canal Zone, where the animals are being recruited for a circus troupe. This will allow for mass scenes of Panaminos, Mesquito and other Indians, tourists, bootleggers and the United States navy, offering an environment of greater variety and more distinctive character than an empty garden.

'The snake we do not like. It is an animal difficult to train and lacking in docility. We propose instead to use a goat.' (SC 109–10)

The statement is also made in various quarters that the war [WWI] represented the eternal conflict of the Zeitgeist with the Zeitschrift. Indeed, a colonel of one of the negro regiments from the United States has said this was exactly his idea in going into it. No doubt it was this idea of a Zeitgeist which inflamed the minds of many of the young men at the time. (SC 115)

MUSSOLINI REFORMS BASEBALL

CHICAGO, Thursday. – Signor Mussolini, during his visit to Chicago, witnessed a baseball game for the first time. The great Italian patriot expressed himself as delighted with the contest which he declares to be the nearest thing to the true Fascisti idea that he has seen in America.

He admired especially the rigidity and stringency of the rules, but questions whether there are enough of them. At present, he says, it would be possible to know all the rules, whereas in Italy the rules of any public game are kept secret. He was surprised to find that the umpire has no power of life and death over the players. (SC 126)

∽

II
(From a Young Peoples' Encyclopedia of Useful Knowledge, A.D. 4026)

The dog (pronounced dog, or perhaps dorg; some authorities prefer dawg): An extinct carnivorous mammalian quadruped of the late Grammoradial Age. It lived partly on human trousers and partly on refuse such as beefsteak, lamb chops, and deviled kidneys.

Owing to its savageness and ferocity, the Dog was in great demand with our ancestors. In the days when the habit of living was in single families in isolated houses, often separated from all other dwellings by iron railings, the dog was of the greatest value in keeping unsolicited visitors at a distance. (See under *Book Agent and Canvasser*; see also the article on *Life Insurance*.)

Of the various kinds or breed of dogs thus maintained, we may mention the terrier, used for biting the ankles; the hound, used for pursuing pedestrians; the Bull Dog, for eating tramps; and the Lap Dog, for indoor biting. In addition to these, the Great Dane, used by the rich for biting the poor, may be mentioned along with the Mongrel, used by the poor for biting the rich.

From contemporary records we learn that persons who attached themselves to a Dog developed the greatest fidelity towards it, following it around all day, and walking great distances after it, often through broken country. Before the era of flying, it is said that Dog-Walking was a familiar pastime, every Dog permitting himself to be accompanied by one, two, or even more persons.

III
THE HOUSE-FLY
(From the Same Authority)

The House-Fly (not to be confused with the Bat, the Hornet, and other household pets of the same epoch) appears to have been a prime favorite with our ancestors. The bright, merry ways of the little fellow, his shiny coat, his glossy wings, and his large eyes twinkling with merriment, endeared him to the household. No household, in fact, was complete, at least in the bright season of summer without its complement of the cheery little fellows, buzzing against the window-panes, or sitting floating on the milk.

Fly-raising usually began in the spring. The careful housewife set out large cans filled with what was called at that epoch Garbage (see under *Garbage in the Twentieth Century*; see also under *Salad, Mixed Grill, and Hash*) placed in sunny corners and liberally coated with fly-eggs, collected by sweeping up the accumulated dust in the corners and angles of the room. A trained housekeeper thus raised anywhere from one to ten thousand flies in a season.

As recently as one hundred years ago, the fly needed, it would seem, but little sleep, and during the night would sit beside his master's bed, ready to call him at the first light of dawn by a playful buzzing in his ear. Surly indeed was the sluggard who could resist the little fellow's winsome invitation to come out and chase him on the lawn.

The care and raising of the Fly occupied a large part of the time of the women-folk of our ancestors. A fly is reported to have been seen alive, sitting on one of the piles of a pier in the Hudson River, looking disconsolately at the water. Since that time the Fly is only found in the museum. There is a good Fly in the famous Morgan collection and there are two in the British Museum. (SC 148–9)

With the exception of the house fly, the mosquito is perhaps the most widely disseminated of our domesticated insects. He is to be found almost anywhere on verandas, or upper and lower balconies, on front and back steps; but he is seen at his best when tucked away behind the little white bed curtains that are specially provided for him.

It is here that he can most successfully be brought to hand-to-hand conflict, which is his delight.

A mosquito, as seen under a microscope, is, to the naturalist, an object of unequalled delight. His four pair of eyes with double refracting lenses from which the light glitters in all directions are equaled only by the great sweep of his gossamer wings and the beautiful articulation of his sixteen legs.

Most striking of all is his powerful bill, armed on each side with teeth, like a double crosscut saw, with which he bores through the cranium of his enemy. The mosquito knows no half measures. He is out for blood. Hence comes his high personal courage which enables him to attack single-handed and unsupported an opponent of twenty thousand times his own weight.

Odds are nothing to him. He rushes into battle singing as he goes, selects the stoutest of his enemies, and seizes him in a death grip in the fattest part of his neck. The British bull-dog and the American eagle are cowards beside the mosquito.

Protection against the assaults of the mosquito has always presented a serious problem to the settlers and campers in our summer wildernesses. But by the trained naturalist, or nature lover, the difficulty is easily overcome.

The naturalist before setting out on his study smears himself with ham fat and oil of citronella, over which he spreads a thin layer of beeswax and asafetida. He then sprays his clothes with coal oil and drapes himself from the head down in a long white net. Thus prepared the naturalist need fear nothing outside of Bengal.

It is a pity to think that the mosquito, like the house fly, is threatened with extinction. There are said to be only a few billion million left. Even these are going – falling victims to their own high courage in their fierce assaults against our civilization like the Crusaders dashing against the Saracens.

But no doubt the efforts of the new Mosquito Preservation Society, one of the latest of our animal philanthropy efforts, will induce the government to step in before it becomes too late. A suitable reservation of land as a Mosquito Park may preserve for our descendants a few thousand million specimens of what was once the dominant animal of North America. (SC 165–6)

'Margaret Overproof was neither short nor tall. Her perfect figure, slender and at the same time fat, conveyed at times an impression of commanding height while at other times she looked sawed off. Her complexion, which was of the tint of a beautiful dull marble like the surface of a second-hand billiard ball, was shot at times with streaks of red and purple which almost suggested apoplexy. Her nose which was clear-cut and aquiline was at the same time daintily turned up at the end and then moved off sideways. A critic might have considered her mouth a trifle too wide and her lips a trifle too full, but on the other hand a horse buyer would have considered them all right. Her eyes were deep and mournful and lit with continuous merriment. Her graceful neck sloped away in all directions till it reached her bust, which stopped it.' (SC 192)

And all the time I was wondering who he was. I didn't know him from Adam: I couldn't recall him a bit. I don't mean that my memory is weak. On the contrary, it is singularly tenacious. True, I find it very hard to remember people's *names*; very often too it is hard for me to recall a *face*; and frequently I fail to recall a person's appearance; and of course clothes are a thing one doesn't notice. But apart from these details, I never forget anybody and I am proud of it. (BB 54–5)

OTHER NATIONS

They [the Irish] make a Constitutional Amendment Act of their own (1936). By this the British King is King of Ireland; but not King of Ireland in Ireland, only outside of it. To find the solution, turn to the back of the book. That's the sole connection of Ireland with the Empire, except its language. Even as to that, they're working hard to restore the old Gaelic. If they're not careful, they'll learn to speak it and then they'll be sorry. (LaL 53–4)

First, the imaginary Frenchman, still seen on the comic stage and still used as the basis of the world's politics; always called Alphonse or Gaston; wears a bell-shaped coat; eats frogs; prefers other men's wives to his own; good taste but no morals. (HML 6)

... the imaginary Irishman; always saying 'Arrah' and 'Macushla' and 'Mavourneen'; always ready for a fight; no respect for the law; makes a fine policeman. (HML 6–7)

... the Scotchman. I lean towards him, but not from any point of descent. I have no Scotch in me except what I put in. But you know that imaginary Scotchman who, I will say, has perhaps kept his national characteristics more stubbornly than the others; very hard, very dour; believes in hell – hopes to go there; looks on any other place as not economical enough. (HML 7)

❧

I am quite familiar with other people's chapters on 'The Mind of America,' and 'The Chinese Mind,' and so forth. Indeed, so far as I know it has turned out that almost everybody all over the world has a mind. Nobody nowadays [ca. 1922] travels, even in Central America or Tibet, without bringing back a chapter on 'The Mind of Costa Rica,' or on the 'Psychology of the Mongolian.' Even the gentler peoples such as the Burmese, the Siamese, the Hawaiians, and the Russians, though they have no minds are written up as souls. (MDE 46–7)

❧

To express the situation in Irish, the more you think of its future, the less you think of it. (HTT 256)

❧

The passion to be left alone, if only to one's own foolishness, lies deep rooted in the British character. (HL 29)

❧

German settlers in America lay like an inert mass, waiting, with beer and music, for someone to turn them into something else. They might have coagulated into Nazis, as nature breeds horse-flies. Luckily they didn't know it. They turned instead into solid American Republicans and Canadian liberals. (BE 26)

❧

The United States ... came into its own as the new home of ... 'equality,' outspoken and even braggart and vulgar ... but still equality. (HL 43, final ellipsis in original)

⁂

Life there [the Soviet Union], from what I can gather at a distance of six thousand miles, – which is all I propose to gather – seems in some way – how shall I say it, restrained, what one might call un-homelike. (OF 152)

⁂

In the first place it must be admitted that the Scotch are a trouble-some people. I do not say that persecution is good for the Scotch, but it may be doubted whether it is bad for them. (ELS 308)

⁂

'Let me tell you, then,' I said, 'that I am an anarchistic polygamist, that I am opposed to all forms of government, that I object to any kind of revealed religion, that I regard the state and property and marriage as the mere tyranny of the bourgeoisie, and that I want to see class hatred carried to the point where it forces everyone into brotherly love. Now, do I get in?'

The official [British Customs] looked puzzled for a minute. 'You are not Irish, are you, sir?' he said.

'No.'

'Then I think you can come in all right,' he answered. (MDE 24)

⁂

It was a gloriously beautiful Scotch morning. The rain fell softly and quietly, bringing dampness and moisture, and almost a sense of wet-ness to the soft moss underfoot. Grey mists flew hither and thither, carrying with them an invigorating rawness that had almost a feeling of dampness.

It is the memory of such a morning that draws a tear from the eye of Scotchmen after years of exile. The Scotch heart, reader, can be moved to its depths by the sight of a raindrop or the sound of a wet rag. (NN 96)

❀

It had been six generations agone at a Highland banquet, in the days when the unrestrained temper of the time gave way to wild orgies, during which theological discussions raged with unrestrained fury. Shamus McShamus, an embittered Calvinist, half crazed perhaps with liquor, had maintained that damnation could be achieved only by faith. Whimper McWhinus had held that damnation could be achieved also by good works. Inflamed with drink McShamus had struck McWhinus across the temple with an oatcake and killed him. (NN 98)

❀

Who were the [liquor] license commissioners, anyway? Why, look at the license system they had in Sweden; yes, and in Finland and in South America. Or, for the matter of that, look at the French and Italians, who drink all day and all night. Aren't they all right? Aren't they a musical people? Take Napoleon, and Victor Hugo; drunk half the time, and yet look what they did. (SS 17–18)

❀

Even on these terms the child is not a success. It has a rival who is rapidly beating it off the ground. This is the Parisian dog. As an implement of fashion, as a set-off to the fair sex, as the recipient of ecstatic kisses and ravishing hugs, the Parisian dog can give the child forty points in a hundred and win out. It can dress better, look more intelligent, behave better, bark better – in fact, the child is simply not in it.

This is why, I suppose, in the world of Parisian luxury, the dog is ousting the infant altogether. You will see, as I said, no children on the boulevards and avenues. You will see dogs by the hundred. Every motor or open barouche that passes up the Champs Elysées, with its little white cloud of fluffy parasols and garden-hats, has a dainty, beribboned dog sitting among its occupants; in every avenue and

promenade you will see hundreds of clipped poodles and toy span-
iels; in all the fashionable churches you will see dogs bowed at their
devotions.

It was a fair struggle. The child had its chance and was beaten.
The child couldn't dress: the dog could. The child couldn't or
wouldn't pray: the dog could, or at least he learnt how. No doubt it
came awkwardly at first, but he set himself to it till nowadays a
French dog can enter a cathedral with just as much reverence as his
mistress, and can pray in the corner of the pew with the same humil-
ity as hers. When you get to know the Parisian dogs, you can easily
tell a Roman Catholic from a Low Church Anglican. I knew a dog
once that was converted – everybody said from motives of policy –
from a Presbyterian – but, stop, it's not fair to talk about it, the dog
is dead now, and it's not right to speak ill of its belief, no matter how
mistaken it may have been.

However, let that pass, what I was saying was that between the
child and the dog, each had its chance in a fair open contest and the
child is nowhere. (BB 82–3)

The 'approaching marriage' referred of course to Dr. Dumfarthing's
betrothal to Juliana Furlong. It was not known that he had ever
exactly proposed to her. But it was understood that before giving up
his charge he drew her attention, in very severe terms, to the fact
that, as his daughter was now leaving him, he must either have
someone else to look after his manse or else be compelled to incur
the expense of a paid housekeeper. This latter alternative, he said,
was not one that he cared to contemplate. He also reminded her that
she was now at a time of life when she could hardly expect to pick
and choose and that her spiritual condition was one of at least great
uncertainty. These combined statements are held, under the law
of Scotland at any rate, to be equivalent to an offer of marriage.
(AA 137–8)

Without wishing in any way to disturb international relations, one cannot help noticing the rough and inquisitorial methods of the English customs men as compared with the gentle and affectionate ways of the American officials at New York. The two trunks that I brought with me [to England] were dragged brutally into an open shed, the strap of one of them was rudely unbuckled while the lid of the other was actually lifted at least four inches. The trunks were then roughly scrawled with chalk, the lids slammed to, and that was all. Not one of the officials seemed to care to look at my things or to have the politeness to pretend to want to. I had arranged my dress suit and my pajamas so as to make as effective a display as possible: a New York customs officer would have been delighted with it. Here they simply passed it over. 'Do open this trunk,' I asked one of the officials, 'and see my pajamas.' 'I don't think it is necessary, sir,' the man answered. There was a coldness about it that cut me to the quick. (MDE 23)

The climate of London and indeed of England generally is due to the influence of the Gulf Stream. The way it works is thus: The Gulf Stream, as it nears the shores of the British Isles and feels the propinquity of Ireland, rises into the air, turns into soup, and comes down on London. At times the soup is thin and is in fact little more than a mist: at other times it has the consistency of a thick Potage St. Germain. (MDE 45)

It [the Irish question ca. 1922] is settled. A group of Irish delegates and British ministers got together round a table and settled it. The settlement has since been celebrated at a demonstration of brotherhood by the Irish Americans of New York with only six casualties. Henceforth the Irish question passes into history. There may be some odd fighting along the Ulster border, or a little civil war with perhaps a little revolution every now and then, but as a question the thing is finished. (MDE 66)

I find that, classified altogether, there are seventeen reasons advanced in Scotland for taking whisky. They run as follows: Reason one, because it is raining; Two, because it is not raining; Three, because you are just going out into the weather; Four, because you have just come in from the weather; Five – no, I forget the ones that come after that. But I remember that reason number seventeen is 'because it canna do ye any harm.' On the whole, reason seventeen is the best.

Put in other words this means that the Scotch make use of whisky with dignity and without shame: and they never call it alcohol. (MDE 138)

I find that, classified altogether, there are seventeen reasons advanced in Scotland for taking whisky. They run as follows: Reason one, because it is raining; Two, because it is not raining; Three, because you are just going out into the weather; Four, because you have just come in from the weather; Five – no, I forget the ones that come after that. But I remember that reason number seventeen is 'because it canna do ye any harm.' On the whole, reason seventeen is the best.

The Scotch, by the way, resemble us in liking to tell and hear stories. But they have their own line. They like the stories to be grim, dealing in a jocose way with death and funerals. The story begins (will the reader kindly turn it into Scotch pronunciation for himself), 'There was a Sandy MacDonald had died and the wife had the body all laid out for burial and dressed up very fine in his best suit,' etc. Now for me that beginning is enough. To me that is not a story, but a tragedy. I am so sorry for Mrs. MacDonald that I can't think of anything else. But I think the explanation is that the Scotch are essentially such a devout people and live so closely within the shadow of death itself that they may without irreverence or pain jest where our lips would falter. Or else, perhaps they don't care a cuss whether Sandy MacDonald died or not. Take it either way. (MDE 193–4)

Mutilated by school recitations, massacred at a thousand pianos, the words still haunt, the melodies still sound. The reason is that [Thomas] Moore's work was wonderfully and typically Irish – the wistful regret for things that have been and are not, regret that things must ever end, or that they don't begin, a kind of satisfied dissatisfaction with life. Said in English it sounds like grumbling. Said in Irish it is called a 'lament' and connects somehow with the pathos of natural scenery and the rippling music of words. (RU 164)

✍

The British are an odd people. They have their own ways and they stick to them; and I like every one of them.

They have their own way of talking. When an Englishman has anything surprising to tell he never exaggerates it, never overstates it – in fact he makes as little of it as possible. And a Scotchman doesn't even mention it. An Englishman can speak of a play of Shakespeare as 'rather good,' and of grand opera as 'not half bad.' He can call Haile Selassie a 'rather decent little chap,' and the President of the United States a 'thoroughly good sort.' (RU 186)

✍

The British Empire [ca. 1944] covers one quarter of the globe (13,353,000 square miles) and includes about on quarter (525,000,000) of its inhabitants. It's a pity it's not bigger ...

Constitutionally, the Empire is supposed to be held together by the Statute of Westminster, a British Imperial statute of 1931. But that's just a 'suppose.' In reality, it is just held together by a vast gentlemen's agreement, and in the case of Ireland it isn't even gentlemanly. (LaL 53)

OTHER WRITERS

I know there are solid arguments advanced in favour of the classics. I often hear them from my colleagues. My friend the professor of Greek tells me that he truly believes the classics have made him what he is. This is a very grave statement, if well founded. Indeed, I have heard the same argument from a great many Latin and Greek scholars. They all claim, with some heat, that Latin and Greek have practically made them what they are. This damaging charge against the classics should not be too readily accepted. In my opinion some of these men would have been what they are, no matter what they were. (BB 122)

This is what I should like to do. I'd like to take a large stone and write on it in very plain writing –

'The classics are only primitive literature. They belong to the same class as primitive machinery and primitive music and primitive medicine,' and then throw it through the windows of a University and hide behind a fence to see the professors buzz! (BB 125)

Or let me take another example from the so-called *Catalogue of the Ships* that fills up nearly an entire book of Homer. This famous passage names all the ships, one by one, and names the chiefs who sailed on them, and names the particular town or hill or valley that they came from. It has been much admired. It has that same majesty of style that has been brought to an even loftier pitch in the *New York Business Directory* and the *City Telephone Book*. (BB 124)

✑

[Aristophanes is] so witty that it takes half a page to explain one of his jokes. (HTT 15)

✑

[Chaucer] told dirty stories well. (HTT 247)

✑

In effect, Shakespeare, instead of sitting down and making up a play out of his head, appears to have rummaged among sagas, myths, legends, archives and folk lore, much of which must have taken him years to find ... In person Shakespeare is generally represented as having a pointed beard and bobbed hair, with a bald forehead, large wide eyes, a salient nose, a retreating chin and a general expression of vacuity, verging on imbecility. (WW 6)

✑

And what is more, even appreciation with the lapse of years may shift from its true basis to a false. Shakespeare is admired now, by the high-brows, for things he never thought of, for effects he never planned. Scholars dissect Chaucer and sew him up again all full of 'purpose.' The college taxidermists have whole museums full of stuffed authors. In the end it doesn't matter. Native appreciation lives on after the stuffing has fallen out. (RU 59)

✑

[Molière is] a genius head and shoulders above his time. (HTT 15)

✑

Schopenhauer has told us ... that all those concepts are amusing in which there is the subsumption of a double paradox. This is a proposition which none of us will readily deny, and one which, if more widely appreciated, might prove of the highest practical utility. (ELS 101)

✍

Kant, likewise, has said that in him everything excites laughter in which there is a resolution or deliverance of the absolute captive by the finite. It was very honourable of Kant to admit this. It enables us to know exactly what did, and what did not, excite him. (ELS 101)

✍

[Dickens] did as much as, or more than, all the Benthams and the Romillys and the Shaftesburys to sweep away the removable hardships, the cruelties and injustices of the England of his day. He led where legislation followed. The pen was mightier than the parliament. (HTT 118–19)

✍

[Mr. Wackford Squeers of Dickens's *Nicholas Nickleby*] did more to reform the gross incompetence and brutality of English People's schools than volumes of inspectors' reports. (CD 52)

✍

It is of no consequence whether *A Christmas Carol* is true to life. It is better than life. (CD 110–11)

✍

The chief and most obvious personal characteristic of the Reverend Charles Dodgson [penname Lewis Carroll] was his extraordinary fondness for little girls; he loved to loll with them in punts, to nestle with them in the grass beneath a tree, and to tell them never-ending stories. This is of course so admirable, especially in a young cleric, that those of us made of rougher metal are not allowed to call it 'sissy.' But I'd like to – the endless pussy-wussy letters to little girls,

the endless willingness to have them in to tea, and to take their pho-
tographs in the spacious set of rooms which he enjoyed at Christ
Church. A little of that sort of thing may be excellent but, as they
say in Yiddish-English, too much is enough. (LaL 166)

Hence W.S. Gilbert was already quite a celebrity in London long
before the Gilbert and Sullivan operas turned celebrity to glory. But
in a way it was not altogether an enviable celebrity. Gilbert from
all accounts was a singularly disagreeable man, self-important and
domineering, rating everybody else as poor trash. By good rights,
great humourists ought to be gentle, agreeable people to meet, with
a breadth of view and a kindly tolerance of trifles – such as they
show in print. Mostly they are not. Charles Dickens, in spite of a
boundless energy and exuberance of fun, was an intolerable egotist
who had to be 'it' all the time, who supplied sob-words and slow
music for the fathers of broken homes and smashed his own with
an axe. Mark Twain, though good, easy company when young,
became, so some people tell us, intolerably boring in old age. Lewis
Carroll was a sissy, and Gilbert was a bully, over conscious of his
own talent. (LaL 192)

Ever so many people have tried to imitate Lewis Carroll and failed.
But the first one who tried and failed was Lewis Carroll himself
[with *Sylvie and Bruno* in 1889]. (LaL 189)

[Mark Twain] was able, under the guise of humour, to give vent
to the fierce elemental ideas of justice and right and equality, hatred
of oppression and religious persecution, by which he was inspired.
(MT 105–6)

Reduced to a simple formula, as it often is, [Alphonse] Daudet's picture of the 'midi' is made to read that in Southern France all the people lie and exaggerate and bluff. That isn't it at all. Like all formulas it perverts truth by condensation. What Daudet meant was that in the South they live in a super-world, like children playing games: a world where they can believe anything they want to believe, and where emphasis lies not on actuality but on appearance: not on whether a thing is or is not so (a matter of no consequence), but on how it sounds. (HH 149)

Dickens' creation of Mr. Pickwick did more for the elevation of the human race – I say it in all seriousness – than Cardinal Newman's *Lead, Kindly Light, Amid the Encircling Gloom.* Newman only cried out for light in the gloom of a sad world. Dickens gave it. (FF 310–11)

Unfortunately our American college-bred authors [historians] cannot be flippant if they try: it is at best but the lumbering playfulness of the elephant, humping his heavy posteriors in the air and wiggling his little tail in the vain attempt to be a lamb. (ELS 86)

Those who can remember their first shock of pleased surprise on hearing that Rudyard Kipling's name was really Rudyard Kipling, will feel something like pain in learning that any writer could deliberately christen himself 'O. Henry.' (ELS 238)

All through this period Canadian militant politics were illustrated and enlivened by the genius of J.W. Bengough whose cartoons in his weekly *Grip* became a national feature, never attempted before, never achieved since. This tendency to turn our politics into fun we

share with the Americans. Its influence for good has been incalcula-
ble. This is a digression, but the memory of Bengough is worth it.
(CFF 191)

Her [poet Eliza Cook's] Red Indian – exact location not specified –
lives quietly in his 'maize-covered grounds' under a 'date-shadowed
roof.' Presumably the dates are 1492 and that of the Louisiana Pur-
chase, 1803, things that must have shadowed Indian life. (HTW 199)

It was one of those regular poets with a solemn jackass face, and lank
parted hair and eyes like puddles of molasses. (SS 104–5)

What we particularly like about Ram Spudd, and we do not say this
because we discovered him but because we believe it and must say it,
is that he belongs not to one school but to all of them. As a nature
poet we doubt very much if he has his equal; as a psychologist,
we are sure he has not. As a clear lucid thinker he is undoubtedly
in the first rank; while as a mystic he is a long way in front of it. The
specimens of Mr. Spudd's verse which we append herewith were
selected, we are happy to assure our readers, purely at random from
his work. We first blindfolded ourselves and then, standing with our
feet in warm water and having one hand tied behind our back, we
groped among the papers on our desk before us and selected for our
purpose whatever specimens first came to hand. (MLL 70)

I was grieved to see by the papers a few weeks ago that the world has
lost that kindly Irish poet, W.B. Yeats. I knew him a little bit, years
ago. Unlike most literary celebrities, he looked the part. His face
would assume at times a look of far-away abstraction, such as only a
poet would wear.

One time when 'Billy' Yeats was in Montreal lecturing, I gave a supper party for him at the University Club – a large round table filled with admiring women, and silent husbands. There came a lull in the conversation during which Yeats' face assumed the far-away look of which I speak. The ladies gazed at him in rapt admiration. At last one said:

'What are you thinking about, Mr. Yeats?'

'Thinking of tomorrow,' he answered in his rich musical voice, 'and wondering!'

You could feel the ripple of sympathetic interest among the ladies: the word 'tomorrow' carries such infinite meaning.

'Wondering what?' someone ventured in a half whisper.

'Wondering,' said Yeats, 'if there is breakfast on the Boston train.' (TMC 200)

∽

It was in Montreal away back in 1902 or 1901 – at any rate in the year, whichever it was, when Émile Zola died.

I had gone into the bar of the old Prince of Wales Hotel to get a drink before dinner, and stood reading the evening paper while I drank it.

My eye suddenly caught a news item and I looked up – forgetting in my surprise just who I was talking to – and said to the bartender.

'Billy, you don't mean to tell me that Émile Zola's dead?'

Billy shook his head sadly and went on wiping the bar with his cloth as he said:

'I think he must be. I ain't seen him round anyway for a week or more.' (TMC 201–2)

∽

I knew [Thorstein] Veblen well. He taught me at Chicago thirty-eight years ago when I was a graduate student in economics. Veblen had a beautiful and thoughtful mind, free from anger and dispute, and heedless of all money motive. As a lecturer he had no manner, but sat mumbling into his lap, scarcely intelligible. But the words which thus fell into his lap were priceless, and after all Malthus had a hare-lip, Demosthenes stuttered and Oliver Cromwell choked. The ideas of the lectures were gathered later into Veblen's books. The central point of his thought is that human industry is not carried on to satisfy human wants but in order to make money. The two motives do not work, thinks Veblen, to a single end as Adam Smith and John Stuart Mill had thought they do. They fall apart. Hence a lot of people get too much money. These have to find ways of spending it in 'conspicuous consumption.' This is the 'leisure class,' a sort of flower on a manure heap. (MDW 136–7)

The new movement [of the 1860s, promoting unrestricted trade reciprocity with the USA] had behind it the powerful support of the illustrious Goldwin Smith, then living in Toronto, an Oxford scholar of such eminence that he could agree with no one but himself, who found England too English and the United States too American. His participation in the foundation of Cornell University (after the Civil War) he had abandoned, still in the heat of the day. He now lived in retirement in his Toronto Grange, the patronizing patron of Canadian culture. His independent fortune heightened the independence of his mind, but narrowed its outlook. His biographer tells us how Goldwin Smith stood one day at his drawing-room window, overlooking the grounds of the Grange, musing on the reported strikes and violence at Cripple Creek. 'Why can't people be content,' he murmured, 'with what they have?' Why not? He himself, in property and investments, had close to a million. (CFF 191–2)

PARODY

The Victorians needed parody. Without it their literature would have been a rank and weedy growth, over-watered with tears. A lot of their writing called aloud for parody. (HH 71)

The Great Detective sat in his office ... Half a bucket of cocaine and a dipper stood on a chair at his elbow. (NN 16)

With the Great Detective, to think was to act, and to act was to think. Frequently he could do both together. (NN 19)

Lord Ronald said nothing; he flung himself from the room, flung himself upon his horse and rode madly off in all directions. (NN 54)

On the fourth day a pirate ship appeared. Reader, I do not know if you have ever seen a pirate ship. The sight was one to appall the stoutest heart. The entire ship was painted black, a black flag hung at the masthead, the sails were black, and on the deck people dressed all in black walked up and down arm-in-arm. The words 'Pirate Ship' were painted in white letters on the bow. At the sight of it our crew were visibly cowed. It was a spectacle that would have cowed a dog.

The two ships were brought side by side. They were then lashed tightly together with bag string and binder twine, and a gang plank laid between them. In a moment the pirates swarmed upon our deck, rolling their eyes, gnashing their teeth and filing their nails.

Then the fight began. It lasted two hours – with fifteen minutes off for lunch. It was awful. The men grappled with one another, kicked one another from behind, slapped one another across the face, and in many cases completely lost their temper and tried to bite one another. I noticed one gigantic fellow brandishing a knotted towel, and striking right and left among our men, until Captain Bilge rushed at him and struck him flat across the mouth with a banana skin. (NN 116)

∽

This island became my home.

There I eked out a miserable existence, feeding on sand and gravel and dressing myself in cactus plants. Years passed. Eating sand and mud slowly undermined my robust constitution. I fell ill. I died. I buried myself.

Would that others who write sea stories would do as much. (NN 120)

∽

Then later the spring would come and all the plain was bright with flowers and Serge could pick them. Then the rain came and Serge could catch it in a cup. Then the summer cane and the great heat and the storms, and Serge could watch the lightning.

'What is lightning for?' he would ask of Yump, the cook, as she stood kneading the *mush*, or dough, to make *slab*, or pancake, for the morrow. Yump shook her *knob*, or head, with a look of perplexity on her big *mugg*, or face.

'It is God's will,' she said.

Thus Serge grew up a thoughtful child.

At times he would say to his mother, 'Matrinska (little mother), why is the sky blue?' And she couldn't tell him.

Or at times he would say to his father, 'Boob (Russian for father), what is three times six?' But his father didn't know.

Each year Serge grew. (FF 34)

Us Spies or We Spies – for we call ourselves both – are thus a race apart. None know us. All fear us. Where do we live? Nowhere. Where are we? Everywhere. Frequently we don't know ourselves where we are. The secret orders that we receive come from so high up that it is often forbidden to us even to ask where we are. A friend of mine, or at least a Fellow Spy – us Spies have no friends – one of the most brilliant men in the Hungarian Secret Service, once spent a month in New York under the impression that he was in Winnipeg. If this happened to the most brilliant, think of the others. (FrF 15)

Readers are requested to note that this novel [*Spoof: A Thousand-Guinea Novel*] has taken our special prize cheque for a thousand guineas. This alone guarantees for all intelligent readers a palpitating interest in every line of it. Among the thousands of MSS. which reached us – many of them coming in carts early in the morning, and moving in a dense phalanx, indistinguishable from the Covent Garden Market wagons; others pouring down our coal-chute during the working hours of the day; and others again being slipped surreptitiously into our letter-box by pale, timid girls, scarcely more than children, after nightfall (in fact many of them came in their nightgowns) – this manuscript alone was the sole one, in fact the only one, to receive the prize of a cheque of a thousand guineas. To other competitors we may have given, inadvertently perhaps, a bag of sovereigns or a string of pearls, but to this story alone is awarded the first prize by the unanimous decision of our judges ...

This novel represents the last word in up-to-date fiction. It is well known that the modern novel has got far beyond the point of mere story-telling. The childish attempt to *interest* the reader has long since been abandoned by all the best writers. They refuse to do it. The modern novel must convey a message, or else it must paint a picture, or remove a veil, or open a new chapter in human psychology. Otherwise it is no good. *Spoof* does all of these things. The reader rises from its perusal perplexed, troubled, and yet so filled with information that rising itself is a difficulty. (MLL 11–12)

The death of a certain royal sovereign makes it possible for me to divulge things hitherto undivulgeable. Even now I can only tell a part, a small part, of the terrific things that I know. When more sovereigns die I can divulge more. I hope to keep on divulging at intervals for years. But I am compelled to be cautious. My relations with the Wilhelmstrasse, with Downing Street and the Quai d'Orsay, are so intimate, and my footing with the Yildiz Kiosk and the Waldorf-Astoria and Childs' Restaurants are so delicate, that a single *faux pas* might prove to be a false step. (FrF 17)

It appears that the right time to begin gardening is last year. For many things it is well to begin the year before last. For good results one must begin even sooner. Here, for example, are the directions, as I interpret them, for growing asparagus. Having secured a suitable piece of ground, preferably a deep friable loam rich in nitrogen, go out three years ago and plough or dig deeply. Remain a year inactive, thinking. Two years ago pulverize the soil thoroughly. Wait a year. As soon as last year comes set out the young shoots. Then spend a quiet winter doing nothing. The asparagus will then be ready to work at *this* year. (FrF 123–4)

But of course all that kind of thing has drifted into the past. The moving pictures have taken over all the big scenic stuff, and the old melodrama is dead. All that is left for the acting stage now is the

High Brow Drama as I have described it. Even that has got to be made small, delicate – *intimate*, that's the word; I couldn't think of it – what the French call *intime*. The French always go us one better. In the *intime* play there's a minimum of acting and a maximum of thought, very little speaking, or movement or sound. I've worked out a little thing in three brief acts to be used as the final piece of an evening's entertainment. In the first act the characters don't speak at all, they just *brood*. In the second act they are not on the stage at all; it's empty; the effect is that of utter desolation. In the last act they are all dead. I think it will make quite a hit. Good night. (HML 95)

POLITICS

Put into the plainest prose, then, we are saying that the government of every country ought to supply work and pay for the unemployed, maintenance for the infirm and aged, and education and opportunity for the children. (UR 140)

While admitting all the shortcomings and the injustices of the régime under which we have lived [ca. 1919], I am not one of those who are able to see a short and single remedy. Many people when presented with the argument above, would settle it at once with the word 'socialism.' Here, they say, is the immediate and natural remedy. I confess at the outset, and shall develop later, that I cannot view it so. Socialism is a mere beautiful dream, possible only for the angels. The attempt to establish it would hurl us over the abyss. Our present lot is sad, but the frying pan is at least better than the fire. (UR 32)

All must work for the state; only in a socialist commonwealth can social justice be found. There are others, of whom the present writer is one, who see in such a programme nothing but disaster: yet who consider that the individualist principle of 'every man for himself' while it makes for national wealth and accumulated power, favors overmuch the few at the expense of the many, puts an over-great premium upon capacity, assigns too harsh a punishment for easy indolence, and, what is worse, exposes the individual human being too cruelly to the mere accidents of birth and fortune. Under such a system, in short, to those who have is given and from those who have not is taken away even that which they have. (UR 37)

∽

If the day ever comes when we are good enough for such a system [socialism], then we shall need no system at all. (HL 56)

∽

With perfect citizens any government is good. In a population of angels a socialistic commonwealth would work to perfection. But until we have the angels we must keep the commonwealth waiting. (UR 122)

∽

For in the whole program of peaceful socialism there is nothing wrong at all except one thing. Apart from this it is a high and enno-bling ideal truly fitted for a community of saints. And the one thing that is wrong with socialism is that it won't work. That is all. It is, as it were, a beautiful machine of which the wheels, dependent upon some unknown and uninvented motive power, refuse to turn. The unknown motive force in this case means a power of altruism, of unselfishness, of willingness to labor for the good of others, such as the human race has never known, nor is ever likely to know. (UR 94-5)

∽

This socialism, this communism, would work only in Heaven where they don't need it, or in Hell where they already have it. (WLS 51)

∽

The plain assertion that every man looks out for himself (or at best for himself and his immediate family) touches the tender conscience of humanity. It is an unpalatable truth. None the less it is the most nearly true of all the broad generalizations that can be attempted in regard to mankind. (UR 40)

⚬✑

Everybody is either a little liberal or a little conservative of the Gilbert and Sullivan opera. (HL 36)

⚬✑

Modern democracy [is] the best system of government as yet operative in this world of sin. (UR 111)

⚬✑

Good will, the only force in the long run that makes anything politically. (HL 59)

⚬✑

Old-fashioned Tories, like the Duke of Wellington, were reported 'thunderstruck' when they heard of giving a colony its own government. But old-fashioned Tories always are thunderstruck. That's how they live; indignation keeps them warm. (LaL 68)

⚬✑

Till the war [WWII] came we spent our time growling at the imperfections of democracy. Democracy of course was inefficient, so it ought to be. Efficiency is an unnatural strain, like Sunday School, or company manners. Democracy was more or less crooked; so is humanity; so are you.

But democracy was everywhere permeated with humanity, and humour was the very atmosphere of its life. It presented everywhere that rare combination of humbug and sincerity which makes the world go round. It evolved the 'politician' as the master genius of democracy. Chivalry evolved the knight, looking for the Holy Grail. Monarchy evolved the gentleman, hunting foxes. Democracy, in America, evolved the politician, hunting votes. This meant a man who really loved his fellows and could stand for them all day and would give everything to everybody, or promise it, and had no principles that he was not willing to sell for better ones. The politician and our democratic politics moved, if you like, in an atmosphere of humbug, of make-believe anger, and mock denunciation. A politician could boil with indignation, as easily as an egg on a heater. He would stand appalled at anything he needed to stand appalled at. The country was alternately saved or lost every two years, it moved on the brink of ruin, it rounded a corner, it emerged into sunlight – something doing all the time. But with it all how utterly and vastly superior it has been to anything that despotism can ever offer to Europe. (RU 102–3)

I think it [provincial debt] can be brought down, to within tolerable limits, by means that are not extraordinary or revolutionary but, reasonable, and if the word is not offensive, conservative. (MDW 86–7)

As to the profiteer, bring him back [ca. 1922]. He is really just the same person who a few years ago was called a Captain of Industry and an Empire Builder and a Nation Maker. It is the times that have changed, not the man. He is there still, just as greedy and rapacious as ever, but no greedier: and we have just the same social need of his greed as a motive power in industry as we ever had, and indeed a worse need than before ... And incidentally, when the profiteer has finished his work, we can always put him back into the penitentiary if we like. But we need him just now. (MDE 129–30)

In and of itself, a vote is nothing. It neither warms the skin nor fills the stomach. Very often the privilege of a vote confers nothing but the right to express one's opinion as to which of two crooks is the crookeder. (ELS 150)

I suppose in a sense we are all brothers. So are the monkeys. (SC 147)

It was not just clear how and where this movement of indignation had started. People said that it was part of a new wave of public morality that was sweeping over the entire United States. Certainly it was being remarked in almost every section of the country. Chicago newspapers were attributing its origin to the new vigour and the fresh ideals of the middle west. In Boston it was said to be due to a revival of the grand old New England spirit. In Philadelphia they called it the spirit of William Penn. In the south it was said to be the reassertion of southern chivalry making itself felt against the greed and selfishness of the north, while in the north they recognized it at once as a protest against the sluggishness and ignorance of the south. In the west they spoke of it as a revolt against the spirit of the east and in the east they called it a reaction against the lawlessness of the west. But everywhere they hailed it as a new sign of the glorious unity of the country. (AA 141–2)

Mr. Fyshe, as chairman, addressed the meeting. He told them they were there to initiate a great free voluntary movement of the people. It had been thought wise, he said, to hold it with closed doors and to keep it out of the newspapers. This would guarantee the league against the old underhand control by a clique that had hitherto disgraced every part of the administration of the city. He wanted, he said, to see everything done henceforth in broad daylight: and for this purpose he had summoned them there at night to discuss ways and means of action. After they were once fully assured of exactly what they wanted to do and how they meant to do it, the league he said, would invite the fullest and freest advice from all classes in the city. There were none, he said, amid great applause, that were so lowly that they would not be invited – once the platform of the league was settled – to advise and co-operate. All might help, even the poorest. Subscription lists would be prepared which would allow any sum at all, from one to five dollars, to be given to the treasurer. The league was to be democratic or nothing. The poorest might contribute as little as one dollar: even the richest would not be allowed to give more than five. Moreover he gave notice that he intended to propose that no actual official of the league should be allowed under its by-laws to give anything. He himself – if they did him the honour to make him president as he had heard it hinted was their intention – would be the first to bow to this rule. He would efface himself. He would obliterate himself, content in the interests of all, to give nothing. He was able to announce similar pledges from his friends, Mr. Boulder, Mr. Furlong, Dr. Boomer, and a number of others. (AA 147–8)

Unlike ours, English politics – one hears it on every hand – are pure. Ours unfortunately are known to be not so. The difference seems to be that our politicians will do anything for money and the English politicians won't; they just take the money and won't do a thing for it. (MDE 60)

What I am really trying to say is that all government rests, not on codes and laws (those are for criminals), but on decency, kindly feeling and a proper idea of the merits and rights and the good sides of others. (LaL 62)

For all things in the world the spirit comes first. Liberty can only serve and survive among people worthy of having it. The soul alone can animate the body. (HL 75)

THE PRESS

But even when a journalist has become familiar with all these tricks and tags, the question still remains, can he write? And for this there is no royal academic road, and an alleged training in alleged journalism [one of the above-mentioned tricks being use of the word 'alleged'], if it cuts the student out from a proper share in wider, deeper culture, is dearly bought. (TMC 147)

'There is no doubt that the corruption of the press is one of the worst factors that we have to oppose. But whether we can best fight it by buying the paper itself or buying the staff is hard to say.' (AA 149)

The newspapers did more than this. They printed from day to day such pictures as the portrait of Mr. Fyshe with the legend below, '*Mr. Lucullus Fyshe, who says that government ought to be by the people, from the people, for the people and to the people*'; and the next day another labelled, '*Mr. P. Spillikins, who says that all men are born free and equal*'; and the next day a picture with the words, '*Tract of ground offered for cemetery by Mr. Furlong, showing rear of tanneries, with head of Mr. Furlong inserted.*' (AA 150)

'One day [said the inventor of the first newspaper] we write it out on our sheet "The Grand Turk maketh disastrous war on the Bulgars of the North and hath burnt divers of their villages." And that hath no sooner gone forth than we print another sheet saying, "It would seem that the villages be not burnt but only scorched, nor doth it appear that the Turk burnt them but that the Bulgars burnt divers villages of the Turk and are sitting now in his mosque in the city of Hadrian." Then shall all men run to and fro and read the sheet and question and ask, "Is it thus?" And, "Is it thus?" and by very uncertainty of circumstances, they shall demand the more curiously to see the news sheet and read it.' (MLL 127–8)

Any American reader who studies the English Press [ca. 1922] comes upon these wasted opportunities [to sensationalize] every day. There are indeed certain journals of a newer type which are doing their best to imitate us. But they don't really get it yet. They use type up to about one inch and after that they get afraid.

I hope that in describing the spirit of the English Press I do not seem to be writing with any personal bitterness. I admit that there might be a certain reason for such a bias. During my stay in England I was most anxious to appear as a contributor to some of the leading papers. This is, with the English, a thing that always adds prestige. To be able to call oneself a 'contributor' to *The Times* or to *Punch* or the *Morning Post* or the *Spectator* is a high honour. I have met these 'contributors' all over the British Empire. Some, I admit, look strange. An ancient wreck in the back bar of an Ontario tavern (ancient régime) has told me that he was a contributor to *The Times*: the janitor of the building where I lived admits that he is a contributor to *Punch*: a man arrested in Bristol for vagrancy while I was in England pleaded that he was a contributor to the *Spectator*. In fact, it is an honour that everybody seems to be able to get but me.

I had often tried before I went to England to contribute to the great English newspapers. I had never succeeded. But I hoped that while in England itself the very propinquity of the atmosphere, I mean the very contiguity of the surroundings, would render the attempt easier. I tried and I failed. (MDE 107–8)

The special excellence of *The Times*, as everybody knows, is its fullness of information. For generations past *The Times* has commanded a peculiar minuteness of knowledge about all parts of the Empire. It is the proud boast of this great journal that to whatever faraway, outlandish part of the Empire you may go, you will always find a correspondent of *The Times* looking for something to do. It is said that the present proprietor has laid it down as his maxim, 'I don't want men who think; I want men who know.' The arrangements for thinking are made separately. (MDE 113)

PROFESSORS

The professors whom I see about me to-day [ca. 1923], ordinary quiet men, with the resigned tranquillity that betrays the pathos of intellectual failure – how can I compare them with the intellectual giants to whom I owe everything that I have forgotten. The professors of my college days were scholars, – vast reservoirs of learning, into whose depths one might drop the rope and bucket of curiosity to bring it up full to the brim with the limpid waters of truth. Plumb them? You couldn't. Measure their learning? Impossible. It defied it. They acknowledged it themselves. They taught, – not for mere pecuniary emolument – they despised it – but for the sheer love of learning. And now when I look about me at their successors, I half suspect (it is a hideous thought) that there is a connection between their work and their salaries. (CoD 12–13)

His conversation, even to the tolerant, is impossible. Apparently he has neither ideas nor enthusiasms, nothing but an elaborate catalogue of dead men's opinions which he cites with a petulant and peevish authority that will not brook contradiction, and that must be soothed by a tolerating acquiescence, or flattered by a plenary acknowledgment of ignorance. (ELS 10)

The supreme import of the professor to the students now lies in the fact that he controls the examinations. He holds the golden key which will unlock the door of the temple of learning, – unlock it, that is, not to let the student in, but to let him get out, – into something decent. This fact gives to the professor a fictitious importance, easily confounded with his personality, similar to that of the gate keeper at a dog show, or the ticket wicket man at a hockey match. (ELS 17)

If ever a professor could voice a wish for a change in the methods or aspect of universities, I may say that it often occurs to me that our colleges would be greatly brightened if there were no students; if the professors could saunter undisturbed among the elm trees in friendly colloquy, lecturing – for they know no other form of conversation – to one another; if the library and the campus could enjoy at all seasons the quiet hush that now only falls on them in August; if the deep peace where learning loves to brood were never broken by examinations and roll-calls. (CoD 77–8)

'I should not like to state that of itself mere paralysis need incapacitate a professor. Dr. Thrum, our professor of the theory of music, is, as you know, paralysed in his ears, and Mr. Slant, our professor of optics, is paralysed in his right eye. But this is a case of paralysis of the brain. I fear it is incompatible with professorial work.' (AA 116)

When they have finished their walk across the campus [in the newspaper's comic pages], Gussie and Eddie and Tootsie and Maisie next appear all seated in a terribly comical place called a classroom, taking part in a comical performance called a 'recitation.' This is carried on under the guidance of a 'professor' or 'prof,' and everybody who reads the college press knows exactly what he looks like. He has a bald head and a face like a hard-boiled egg with the shell off, held upside down, and much the same expression as the map of Africa. (SC 78)

❧

But what I failed to meet either on the prairies or the Island [Vancouver] were men of my own particular rank, retired professors. I commented on this at the dinner of which I speak and they told me that there was a retired professor, (also of economics) at the Mental Hospital up at Ulgettit on the Island, (pronounced *you'll get it*). They said I ought to go there. (MDW 193)

❧

Some years ago I was engaged in Montreal in what is called 'historical research,' a thing done by professors in the heart of the summer in the depth of a library where there is no one to check up their time. Often it takes years and years to write a chapter. (MDW 244)

❧

In other words the cart doesn't go before the horse. Not at all. The horse, the mass of human intelligence, draws along the cart of history in which stands the professor, looking backward and explaining the scenery. This is not said unkindly. If he looked forward he wouldn't see any more than the horse does; and the horse sees nothing. (RU 58)

❧

'We shall resume our discussions on Monday,' he said. Being a professor, he knew no other form of farewell. (RU 144)

❧

In other words I am what is called a *professor emeritus* – from the Latin *e*, 'out,' and *meritus*, 'so he ought to be.' (HML 245)

PROGRESS

The record of the age of machinery is known to all. But the strange mystery, the secret that lies concealed within its organization, is realized by but few. It offers, to those who see it aright, the most perplexing industrial paradox ever presented in the history of mankind. With all our wealth we are still poor. After a century and a half of labour-saving machinery, we work about as hard as ever. With a power over nature multiplied a hundred fold, nature still conquers us. And more than this. There are many senses in which the machine age seems to leave the great bulk of civilized humanity, the working part of it, worse off instead of better. (UR 22–3)

The history of invention is the history of applied idleness. To shirk work is to abbreviate labour. To shirk argument is to settle controversy. To shirk war is to cherish peace. (ELS 274)

We have a mean little vanity over our civilisation. We are touchy about it. We do not realise that so far we have done little but increase the burden of work and multiply the means of death. But for the hope of better things to come, our civilisation would not seem worth while. (ELS 146–7)

The melancholy lesson is being learned [ca. 1919] that the path of human progress is arduous and its forward movement slow and that no mere form of government can aid unless it is inspired by a higher public spirit of the individual citizen than we have yet managed to achieve. (UR 114)

I propose, my dear friend, that as a first need for a post-war world you reconstruct yourself a little; shovel up a lot of yourself and throw it away; knock yourself down and start over. And, in particular, cast away a whole lot of minor grievances and mimic animosities that the fierce light of war has brought down to their true pettiness. (LaL 88)

There is no great hope for universal betterment of society by the mere advance of industrial technical progress and by the unaided play of the motive of every man for himself. (UR 85)

The danger is that the attempt to alter things too rapidly may dislocate the industrial machine. We ought to attempt such ... as will strain the machine to a breaking point, but never break it. (UR 149)

The history of our little human race would make but sorry reading were not its every page imprinted with the fact that human ingenuity has invented no torment too great for human fortitude to bear. (ELS 49)

Mechanical progress makes higher wages possible. It does not, of itself, advance them by a single farthing. Labour saving machinery does not of itself save the working world a single hour of toil: it only shifts it from one task to another.

Against a system of unrestrained individualism, energy, industriousness and honesty might shatter itself in vain. The thing is merely a race in which only one can be first no matter how great the speed of all; a struggle in which one, and not all, can stand upon the shoulders of the others. It is the restriction of individualism by the force of organization and by legislation that has brought to the world whatever social advance has been achieved by the great mass of the people. (UR 86)

Altogether I don't know which was best, the little old fair with the hogs and the flowers and Flossie Fitzgerald and the Fat Woman or the Big Show of 1928 with the noise and racket and sputtering fireworks and brain-curdling death stunts.

But I rather suspect that they are much the same thing. Human nature being still human nature, the people of 1880 probably got more or less the same feeling out of it all as we do now. But with that I leave it to the psychoanalysts. (SC 145–6)

The Victorians let the poor starve and shed tears over their graves; we swear at them and feed them. (MDW 148)

RELIGION AND MORALITY

I have noticed that my clerical friends, on the rare occasions when they are privileged to preach to me, have a way of closing their sermons by 'leaving their congregations with a thought.' It is a good scheme. It suggests an inexhaustible fund of reserve thought not yet tapped. It keeps the congregation, let us hope, in a state of trembling eagerness for the next installment. (ELS 159)

I once asked a Christmas Eve group of children if they believed in Santa Claus. The very smallest ones answered without hesitation, 'Why, of course!' The older ones shook their heads. The little girls smiled sadly but said nothing. One future scientist asserted boldly, 'I know who it is'; and a little make-strong with his eye on gain said: 'I believe in it all; I can believe anything.' That boy, I realized, would one day be a bishop. (RU 116)

The pulpit seems for some reason or other to lend itself especially to the creation of mixed metaphors. It may be that the minds of the clergy are filled with the vivid imagery of the scriptures – the green pastures, the fountains, the shadows of great rocks in weary lands, the seeds that grow up to great trees – so filled with them that extempore oratory has not time to sort them out. Hence, we hear them express the hope that the work begun today may kindle a spark which will only need watering to make it a great fire that will spread and multiply till all the fowls of the air can sit on it. (HTW 94)

⌘

The Devil is passing out of fashion. After a long and honourable career he has fallen into an ungrateful oblivion. His existence has become shadowy, his outline attenuated, and his personality dis-pleasing to a complacent generation. So he stands now leaning on the handle of his three-pronged oyster fork and looking into the ashes of his smothered fire. (ELS 41)

⌘

Hell itself was spoken of as She-ol, and it appeared that it was not a place of burning, but rather of what one might describe as moral torment. This settled She-ol once and for all: nobody minds moral torment. (AA 104)

⌘

The vague and hysterical desire to 'uplift' one's self merely for exaltation's sake is about as effective an engine of moral progress as the effort to lift one's self in the air by a terrific hitching up of the breeches. (ELS 52–3)

⌘

We might expect to find, as the general outcome of the new moral code now in the making [ca. 1916], the simple worship of success. This is exactly what is happening. The morality which the Devil with his oyster fork was commissioned to inculcate was essentially altruistic. Things were to be done for other people. The new ideas, if you combine them in a sort of moral amalgam – to develop one's self, to evolve, to measure things by their success – weigh on the other side of the scale. (ELS 58)

⌘

One is apt to suspect that the Victorians felt as if their flood of generous tears washed them free from obligations. (HTW 104)

Yodel, the auctioneer, for example, narrated how he had been to the city and had gone into a service of the Roman Catholic church: I believe, to state it more fairly, he had 'dropped in,' – the only recognized means of access to such a service. He claimed that the music that he had heard there was music, and that (outside of his profession) the chanting and intoning could not be touched. (SS 60–1)

Similarly over at the Presbyterian Church, the minister says that his sacred calling will not allow him to take part in politics and that his sacred calling prevents him from breathing even a word of harshness against his fellow man, but that when it comes to the elevation of the ungodly into high places in the commonwealth (this means, of course, the nomination of the Conservative candidate) then he's not going to allow his sacred calling to prevent him from saying just what he thinks of it. And by that time, having pretty well cleared the church of Conservatives, he proceeds to show from scriptures that the ancient Hebrews were Liberals to a man, except those who were drowned in the flood or who perished, more or less deservedly, in the desert. (SS 119–20)

All of this Mr. Snoop explained in the opening speech which he proceeded to make. And after this he went on to disclose, amid deep interest, the general nature of the cult of Boohooism. He said that they could best understand it if he told them that its central doctrine was that of Bahee. Indeed, the first aim of all followers of the cult was to attain to Bahee. Anybody who could spend a certain number of hours each day, say sixteen, in silent meditation on Boohooism would find his mind gradually reaching a condition of Bahee. The

chief aim of Bahee itself was sacrifice: a true follower of the cult
must be willing to sacrifice his friends, or his relatives, and even
strangers, in order to reach Bahee. In this way one was able fully to
realize oneself and enter into the Higher Indifference. Beyond this,
further meditation and fasting – by which was meant living solely
on fish, fruit, wine, and meat – one presently attained to complete
Swaraj or Control of Self, and might in time pass into the absolute
Nirvana, or the Negation of Emptiness, the supreme goal of Boohooism.

As a first step to all this, Mr. Snoop explained, each neophyte or
candidate for holiness must, after searching his own heart, send
ten dollars to Mr. Yahi-Bahi. Gold, it appeared, was recognized in
the cult of Boohooism as typifying the three chief virtues, whereas
silver or paper money did not; even national banknotes were only
regarded as *dô* or, a halfway palliation; and outside currencies such
as Canadian or Mexican bills were looked upon as entirely *boo*, or
contemptible. The Oriental view of money, said Mr. Snoop, was
far superior to our own, but it also might be attained by deep
thought, and, as a beginning, by sending ten dollars to Mr. Yahi-
Bahi. (AA 68–9)

The ground on which St. Asaph's stands is worth seven dollars and a
half a foot. The mortgagees, as they kneel in prayer in their long
frock-coats, feel that they have built upon a rock. It is a beautifully
appointed church. There are windows with priceless stained glass
that were imported from Normandy, the rector himself swearing out
the invoices to save the congregation the grievous burden of the customs duty. There is a pipe organ in the transept that cost ten thousand dollars to install. The debenture-holders, as they join in the
morning anthem, love to hear the dulcet notes of the great organ
and to reflect that it is a good as new. Just behind the church is St.
Asaph's Sunday School, with a ten-thousand dollar mortgage of its
own. And below that again, on the side street, is the building of the

Young Men's Guild, with a bowling-alley and a swimming-bath deep enough to drown two young men at a time, and a billiard-room with seven tables. It is the rector's boast that with a Guild House such as that there is no need for any young man of the congregation to frequent a saloon. Nor is there. (AA 101)

∽

St. Osoph's is only Presbyterian in a special sense. It is, in fact, too Presbyterian to be any longer connected with any other body whatsoever. It seceded some forty years ago from the original body to which it belonged, and later on, with three other churches, it seceded from the group of seceding congregations. Still later it fell into a difference with the other churches on the question of eternal punishment, the word 'eternal' not appearing to the elders of St. Osoph's to designate a sufficiently long period. The dispute ended in a secession which left the church of St. Osoph's practically isolated in a world of sin whose approaching fate it neither denied nor deplored. (AA 102)

∽

Whatever sin there was in the City was shoved sideways into the roaring streets of commerce where the elevated railway ran, and below that again into the slums. Here there must have been any quantity of sin. The rector of St. Asaph's was certain of it. Many of the richer of his parishioners had been down in parties late at night to look at it, and the ladies of his congregation were joined together into all sorts of guilds and societies and bands of endeavour for stamping it out and driving it under or putting it into jail till it surrendered.

But the slums lay outside the rector's parish. He had no right to interfere. (AA 108)

∽

Thus slowly and with many interruptions the [Episcopalian] rector

made his progress along the avenue. At times he stopped to permit a
pink-cheeked infant in a perambulator to beat him with a rattle
while he inquired its age of an Episcopal nurse, gay with flowing rib-
bons. He lifted his hat to the bright parasols of his parishioners passing in glistening motors, bowed to Episcopalians, nodded amiably
to Presbyterians, and even acknowledged with his lifted hat the passing of persons of graver forms of error. (AA 109)

'Your items,' said his father [about the minister's accounts book],
'are entered wrongly. Here, for example, in the general statement,
you put down Distribution of Coals to the Poor to your credit. In
the same way, Bibles and Prizes to the Sunday School you again
mark to your credit. Why? Don't you see, my boy, that these things
are debits? When you give out Bibles or distribute fuel to the poor
you give out something for which you get no return. It is a debit.
On the other hand, such items as Church Offertory, Scholars' Pennies, etc., are pure profit. Surely the principle is clear ... Anything
which we give out without return or reward we count as a debit; all
that we take from others without giving in return we count as so
much to our credit.' (AA 112–13)

The older way of being good was by much prayer and much effort
of one's own soul. Now it is done by a Board of Censors. There is no
need to fight sin by the power of the spirit: let the Board of Censors
do it. They together with three or four kinds of Commissioners are
supposed to keep sin at arm's length and to supply a first-class legislative guarantee of righteousness. As a short cut to morality and as
a way of saving individual effort our legislatures are turning out
morality legislation by the bucketful. The legislature regulates our
drink, it begins already [ca. 1922] to guard us against the deadly cig-
arette, it regulates here and there the length of our skirts, it safe-
guards our amusements and in two states of the American Union it

even proposes to save us from the teaching of the Darwinian theory of evolution. The ancient prayer 'Lead us not into temptation' is passing out of date. The way to temptation is declared closed by Act of Parliament and by amendment to the Constitution of the United States. Yet oddly enough the moral tone of the world fails to respond. The world is apparently more full of thugs, hold-up men, yegg-men, bandits, motor thieves, porch climbers, spotters, spies and crooked policemen than it ever was; till it almost seems that the slow, old-fashioned method of an effort of the individual soul may be needed still before the world is made good. (MDE 126–7)

PEOPLE WHO LIVE IN GLASS HOUSES OUGHT NOT TO THROW STONES

Not at all. *They are the very people who ought to throw stones and to keep on throwing them all the time. They ought to keep up such a fusillade of stones from their glass house that no one can get near it.*

Or if the proverb is taken to mean that people who have faults of their own ought not to talk of other people's faults, it is equally mistaken. They ought to talk of other people's faults all the time so as to keep attention away from their own. (WW 61)

But the moralist – that's me – is bound to ask where is it leading us? What is the result of it on our minds and characters, this everlasting dwelling on crime? Somebody wrote long ago that –

Vice is a monster of such hideous mien,
That to be hated needs but to be seen,
But too oft seen, familiar with her face
We first endure, then pity, then embrace.

The same is true of crime. The everlasting depiction and perusal of it corrupts the mind – not yours of course, my dear reader, because you are strong minded. But it corrupts the feeble mind. Personally I admit that I found myself reflecting on the man that killed his mother-in-law and gave no reason and wondering perhaps – but let it go. (WW 116)

For social evils the first remedy is a social consciousness of the evil. If the community becomes conscious of its unwholesome morbid interest in crime, that already will start the cure. Sensible persons here and there will begin to take the mote – or the motor – out of their own eye – as a first step toward taking the beam out of their neighbour's. Newspapers and magazine makers and moving picture makers have no innate desire to foist crime news on the public. They are probably sick of it. Left to themselves they would rather go fishing or dig in the garden. The notion that a newspaper reporter is half brother to the criminal is erroneous. In point of news, and amusements and pictures, the public always gets what the public wants. This is a pity, but it is so. (WW 117)

ROYALTY

To my mind there is something eminently pathetic in the twentieth-century king with his frock coat, his building trowel, his spade, his tree, his statues and the other paraphernalia of his office, his false magnificence and his actual impotence. He is colonel of ten regiments and does not command a single man, the head of a navy and has no power to fire a single gun, wears, in his days of grandeur, twenty uniforms in forty minutes and finds none to fit him. (ELS 292–3)

I'm like that with my underlying Jeffersonian republicanism: back I slip to such crazy ideas as that all men are equal, and that hereditary rights (still saving out the British monarchy) are hereditary wrongs. (BLB 85)

It is a known fact that if a young English Lord comes to an American town he puts it to the bad in one week. Socially the whole place goes to pieces. Girls whose parents are in the hardware business and who used to call their father 'Pop' begin to talk of precedence and whether a Duchess Dowager goes into to dinner ahead of or behind a countess scavenger. (MDE 60)

SCIENCE

What I want to say is that when the scientist steps out from recording phenomena and offers a general statement of the nature of what is called 'reality,' the ultimate nature of space, of time, of the beginning of things, of life, of a universe, then he stands exactly where you and I do, and the three of us stand where Plato did – and long before him Rodin's primitive thinker. (LaL 38)

There followed the researches of the radioactivity school and, above all, those of Ernest Rutherford which revolutionized the theory of matter. I knew Rutherford well as we were colleagues at McGill for seven years. I am quite sure that he had no original intention of upsetting the foundations of the universe. Yet that is what he did, and he was in due course very properly raised to the peerage for it ...

Let us try to show what Rutherford did to the atom. Imagine to yourself an Irishman whirling a shillelagh around his head with the rapidity and dexterity known only in Tipperary or Donegal. If you come anywhere near, you'll get hit with the shillelagh. Now make it go faster; faster still; get it going so fast that you can't tell which is Irishman and which is shillelagh. The whole combination has turned into a green blur. If you shoot a bullet at it, it will probably go through, as there is mostly nothing there. Yet if you go up against it, it won't hit you now, because the shillelagh is going so fast that you will seem to come against a solid surface. Now make the Irishman smaller and the shillelagh longer. In fact, you don't need the Irishman at all; just his force, his Irish determination, so to speak. Just keep that, the *disturbance*. And you don't need the shillelagh either, just the *field of force* that it sweeps. There! Now put in two Irishmen and two shillelaghs and reduce them in the same way to one solid body – at least it seems solid but you can shoot bullets through it anywhere now. What you have now is a hydrogen atom – one proton and one electron flying around as a *disturbance* in space. Put in more Irishmen and more shillelaghs – or, rather, more protons and electrons – and you get other kinds of atoms. Put in a whole lot – eleven protons, eleven electrons; that is a sodium atom. Bunch the atoms together into combinations called molecules, themselves flying round – and there you are! That's solid matter, and nothing in it at all except disturbance. You're standing on it right now: the molecules are beating against your feet. But there is nothing there, and nothing in your feet. This may help you to understand how 'waves,' ripples of disturbance – for instance, the disturbance you call radio – go right through all matter, indeed right through *you*, as if you weren't there. You see, you aren't. (LaL 41–2)

During this very winter [ca. 1929] the most distinguished of British mathematical astronomers has assured the Press that there is life on Mars; that the conditions are such that there cannot fail to be life there. And at the same time a London medical scientist, an expert in radio communication, has announced the receipt of actual messages from the planet.

The announcement has been followed by similar news from other quarters, of messages partly radioactive, and partly telepathic, messages which, of course were imperfect and at times undecipherable, but still, from their very content, undoubtedly messages. To those who have the will to believe and who have not hardened their understandings into scepticism, the thing is achieved. Communication has begun. (IM 138)

SELF-DEVELOPMENT

Here we have first of all the creed and cult of self-development. It arrogates to itself the title of New Thought, but contains in reality nothing but the Old Selfishness. According to this particular outlook the goal of morality is found in fully developing one's self. Be large, says the votary of this creed, be high, be broad. He gives a shilling to a starving man, not that the man may be fed but that he himself may be a shilling-giver. He cultivates sympathy with the destitute for the sake of being sympathetic. The whole of his virtue and his creed of conduct runs to a cheap and easy egomania in which his blind passion for himself causes him to use external people and things as mere reactions upon his own personality. The immoral little toad swells itself to the bursting point in its desire to be a moral ox. (ELS 51–2)

According to all the legends and story books, the principal factor in success is perseverance. Personally, I think there is nothing in it. If anything, the truth lies the other way.

There is an old motto that runs, 'If at first you don't succeed, try, try again.' This is nonsense. It ought to read, 'If at first you don't succeed, quit, quit at once.'

If you can't do a thing, more or less, the first time you try, you will never do it. Try something else while there is yet time. (FrF 132)

He used to ride a bicycle every day to train his muscles and to clear his brain. He looked at all the scenery that he passed to develop his taste for scenery. He gave to the poor to develop his sympathy with poverty. He read the Bible regularly in order to cultivate the faculty of reading the Bible, and visited picture galleries with painful assiduity in order to give himself a feeling for art. He passed through life with a strained and haunted expression waiting for clarity of intellect, greatness of soul, and a passion for art to descend upon him like a flock of doves. He is now dead. He died presumably in order to cultivate the sense of being a corpse. (ELS 53–4)

∽

By the end of his course Edward had reached certain major conclusions. He now saw that Personality is Power; that Optimism opens Opportunity; and that Magnetism Makes Money. He also realized that Harmony makes for Happiness, and that Worry would merely carry his waste products into his ducts and unfit him for success. (GF 21–2)

∽

The Monk or the Good Man of the older day despised the body as a thing that must learn to know its betters. He spiked it down with a hair shirt to teach it the virtue of submission. He was of course very wrong and very objectionable. But one doubts if he was much worse than his modern successor who joys consciously in the operation of his pores and his glands, and the correct rhythmical contraction of his abdominal muscles, as if he constituted simply a sort of superior sewerage system. (ELS 53)

∽

Nor is it only the external aspect of the body that should be an object of continuous attention. The same thing is true of the interior, or what we may call medically, the inside. The prudent man especially as he reaches middle life, will keep a watchful eye turned on his inside. Are his ducts functioning? How is his great colon? And the shorter, or semi-colon, what about that? Is there an easy flow of nitric acid from the esophagus to the proscenium? If not, what is stopping it: has perhaps a lot of sand or mud made its way into the auditorium? Are the sebaceous glands in what one might call efficient working condition, and are the valves of the liver revolving as they ought to? Are the eyes opening and shutting properly, and is the lower jaw swinging on its hinges as it should? In short, the man of discretion will go over himself each day and tap himself with a small hammer to see that his body is functioning as it ought to. (GF 73)

Just now [ca. 1944] we are all filled with the idea of post-war reconstruction, rebuilding the railways, recharting the air, shovelling up the cities. I propose, my dear friend, that as a first need for a post-war world you reconstruct yourself a little; shovel up a lot of yourself and throw it away; knock yourself down and start over. And, in particular, cast away a whole lot of minor grievances and mimic animosities that the fierce light of war has brought down to their true pettiness. (LaL 88)

Try to buy happiness, by the quart or by the yard, and you never find it. Motion it away from you while you turn to Duty and you will find it waiting beside your chair. So with Good Will on Earth. Cannons frighten it. Treaties fetter it. The Spirit brings it. (LaL 107)

SOCIAL JUSTICE

Few persons can attain to adult life without being profoundly impressed by the appalling inequalities of our human lot. Riches and poverty jostle one another upon our streets. The tattered outcast dozes on his bench while the chariot of the wealthy is drawn by. The palace is the neighbor of the slum. We are, in modern life [ca. 1919], so used to this that we no longer see it. (UR 14)

The human mind, lost in a maze of inequalities that it cannot explain and evils that it cannot, singly, remedy, must adapt itself as best it can. An acquired indifference to the ills of others is the price at which we live. A certain dole of sympathy, a casual mite of personal relief is the mere drop that any one of us alone can cast into the vast ocean of human misery. Beyond that we must harden ourselves lest we too perish. We feed well while others starve. We make fast the doors of our lighted houses against the indigent and the hungry. What else can we do? If we shelter one what is that? And if we try to shelter all, we are ourselves shelterless. (UR 15)

In fact, if you were to mount to the roof of the Mausoleum Cub itself on Plutoria Avenue you could almost see the slums from there. But why should you? And on the other hand, if you never went up on the roof, but only dined inside among the palm trees, you would never know that the slums existed – which is much better. (AA 2)

❧

No society is properly organized until every child that is born into it shall have an opportunity in life. Success in life and capacity to live we cannot give. But opportunity we can. We can at least see that the gifts that are laid in the child's cradle by nature are not obliterated by the cruel fortune of the accident of birth: that its brain and body are not stunted by lack of food and air and by the heavy burden of premature toil. The playtime of childhood should be held sacred by the nation. (UR 138–9)

SPECIALIZATION

It is my opinion that now-a-days we are overridden in the specialties, each in his own department of learning, with his tags, and label, and his pigeon-hole category of proper names, precluding all discussion by ordinary people. No man may speak fittingly of the soul without spending at least six weeks in a theological college; morality is the province of the moral philosopher who is prepared to pelt the intruder back over the fence with a shower of German commentaries. Ignorance, in its wooden shoes, shuffles around the portico of the temple of learning, stumbling among the litter of terminology. The broad field of human wisdom has been cut into a multitude of little professorial rabbit warrens. In each of these a specialist burrows deep, scratching out a shower of terminology, head down in an unlovely attitude which places an interlocutor at a grotesque conversational disadvantage. (ELS 44–5)

Botany is the art of plants. Plants are divided into trees, flowers, and vegetables. The true botanist knows a tree as soon as he sees it. He learns to distinguish it from a vegetable by merely putting his ear to it. (LL 75)

The Earth or Globe, on which we collect stamps, is organized by the International Postal Union, which divides it up into countries. The

Postal Union turns on its axis every twenty-four hours, thus creating day and night ...

The Stamp Book can teach us, among other things, the reason and origin of government and how it comes into being. Whenever a part of the earth contains a sufficient number of people to need stamps, the people all get together and join in forming a government the purpose of which is to issue stamps.

If the stamps are to have a man's head as the design, the country is placed under a king, the person selected for the king having the kind of features needed for a stamp. The British Royal family makes such excellent stamps that it is thought that they will be kept at the head of Great Britain for a long time to come. On the other hand, the Emperor of Brazil had to be deposed in 1889, his whiskers being too large to go through the Post. (SC 90)

The prices paid for first editions are no real evidence of the value of a book or the eminence of the author. Indeed the 'first edition' hobby is one of the minor forms of mental derangement, seldom ending in homicide, and outside the scope of the law. (CD 305)

SPIRITUALISM

I do not write what follows with the expectation of convincing or converting anybody. We Spiritualists, or Spiritists – we call ourselves both, or either – never ask anybody to believe us. If they do, well and good. If not, all right. Our attitude simply is that facts are facts. There they are; believe them or not as you like. As I said the other night, in conversation with Aristotle and John Bunyan and George Washington and a few others, why should anybody believe us? Aristotle, I recollect, said that all that he wished was that everybody should know how happy he was; and Washington said that for his part, if people only knew how bright and beautiful it all was where he was, they would willingly, indeed gladly, pay the mere dollar – itself only a nominal fee – that it cost to talk to him. Bunyan, I remember, added that he himself was quite happy. (FrF 40)

I suppose there never was an age more riddled with superstition, more credulous, more drunkenly addicted to thaumaturgy than the present. The Devil in his palmiest days was nothing to it. In despite of our vaunted material common-sense, there is a perfect craving abroad for belief in something beyond the compass of the believable. (ELS 47)

Mrs. Buncomhearst, who had just lost her third husband – by divorce – had received from Mr. Yahi-Bahi a glimpse into the future that was almost uncanny in its exactness. She had asked for a divination, and Mr. Yahi-Bahi had effected one by causing her to lay six ten-dollar pieces on the table arranged in the form of a mystic serpent. Over these he had bent and peered deeply, as if seeking to unravel their meaning, and finally he had given her the prophecy, 'Many things are yet to happen before others begin.' (AA 65)

SPORTING

A sportsman is a man who, every now and then, simply has to get out and kill something. Not that he's cruel. He wouldn't hurt a fly. It's not big enough. (RU 68)

And just one word about fresh air and exercise. Don't bother with either of them. Get your room full of good air, then shut up the windows and keep it. It will keep for years. Anyway, don't keep using your lungs all the time. Let them rest. As for exercise, if you have to take it, take it and put up with it. But as long as you have the price of a hack and can hire other people to play baseball for you and run races and do gymnastics when you sit in the shade and smoke and watch them – great heavens, what more do you want? (LL 25)

I suppose that if I were to keep on yarning like this, some young aspirant to billiard honours would start to ask me about fancy shots and how to do them. For instance, the shot called the *massé* shot is one that always attracts the beginner, but which only the player of long experience need hope to achieve.

In this shot the ball to be hit with the cue is almost touching another ball. The player then, by holding his cue almost vertically in the air, hits downward with such force as to cut a piece out of the cloth of the table.

It is a neat and effective shot, not really as difficult as it looks, but less suited for performance on a public table than for exhibiting to a group of guests on a private table in the host's house. (IM 271)

∽

Here then is a neat subject of calculation. Granted that Jones, – as measured on a hitting machine the week the circus was here, – can hit two tons and that this whole force was pressed against a golf ball only one inch and a quarter in diameter. What happens? My reader will remember that the superficial area of such a golf ball is 3.1415 times 5/4 square inches multiplied by 4, or, more simply, $4PR^2$. And all of this driven forward with the power of 4,000 pounds to the inch!

In short, taking Jones's statements at their face value the ball would have traveled, had it not been for the wind, no less than 6½ miles.

I give the next calculation of even more acute current interest. It is in regard to 'moving the head.' How often is an admirable stroke at golf spoiled by moving the head! I have seen members of our golf club sit silent and glum all evening, murmuring from time to time, 'I moved my head.' When Jones and I play together I often hit the ball sideways into the vegetable garden from which no ball returns (they have one of these on every links; it is a Scottish invention). And whenever I do so Jones always says, 'You moved your head.' In return when *he* drives his ball away up into air and down again ten yards in front of him, I always retaliate by saying, 'You moved your head, old man.'

In short, if absolute immobility of the head could be achieved the major problem of golf would be solved. (SC 40)

∽

THE GOLFER'S POCKET GUIDE ...

Part 1 of the manual is to contain a set of questions and answers framed as an intelligence test. The golf enthusiast, before settling down to his season's work, may test the adjustment of his brain by rapidly running over the following queries:

What is meant by summer?

The time of year during which golf is played.

What other seasons are there?

None, that I can recall.

How would you define a city?

I should call it a large group of houses and people situated within eight or ten miles of a golf club.

Right. And what is a railway?

An apparatus of transportation used as a means of access to a golf club.

What is meant by the country?

Open space about a city divided into golf courses.

If you go further, what do you see?

More golf courses.

Correct. What are trees?

Upright growths of wood on a golf course.

And what is grass?

Vegetation on a fairway. (IM 198–9)

To me, as to ever so many other people, there is singular and abiding charm about fishing. I began it as a little boy, fishing below a mill-dam in the roar and foam of the water. Now, as an old man, I fish above the dam. It's quieter there. That's all the difference ...

My fishing is beside a mill-dam, or the remains of what once was one, a place with old beams and fragments of machinery sticking out in the wreckage of a bygone mill; there or along the banks of the stream that feeds the pond; or better still in a motor boat on a lake that is neither wilderness nor civilization, neither multitude nor solitude, with enough bass in it to keep hope alive and not enough to make continuous trouble. For fishing, as I see it, is in reality not so much an activity as a state of mind. (RU 72–3)

∾

So it may not be without interest to outdoor people – anglers, men of the bush and streams and such – to turn over again the pages of the old volume [*The Compleat Angler*] and see what Izaak Walton can teach us. This, especially, if we can catch something of the leisurely procedure, the old-time courtesy and, so to speak, the charming tediousness of people with lots of time, now lost in our distracted world. (LaL 13)

∾

I wish I could take Hitler and Mussolini out bass fishing on Lake Simcoe [ca. 1939]. They'd come back better men – or they'd never come back. (TMC 243)

∾

Trout, as everyone knows who is an angler, never rise after a rain, nor before one; it is impossible to get them to rise in the heat, and any chill in the air keeps them down. The absolutely right day is a still, cloudy day, but even then there are certain kinds of clouds that prevent a rising of the trout. Indeed I have only to say to one of my expert friends, 'Queer, they didn't bite!' and he's off to a good start with an explanation. There is such a tremendous lot to know about trout-fishing that men who are keen on it can discuss theories of fishing by the hour. (HML 174–5)

∾

You ask perhaps, I hope not with impatience, what we can learn from Izaak Walton. Why, don't you see we've learned a lot already; that fishing is the Apostles' own calling; that fishing must be carried on in an atmosphere of good will and forbearance; that the longest story must never seem prosy; that a cup of ale beneath a tree is better than a civic banquet, and an old familiar song from a familiar singer outclasses grand opera. (LaL 16)

THINKING

A student says 'I want to write'; he never says 'I want to think.' (HTW 3)

The ability to think is rare. Any man can think hard when he has to: the savage devotes a nicety of thought to the equipoise of his club, or the business man to the adjustment of a market price. But the ability or desire to think without compulsion about things that neither warm the hands nor fill the stomach, is very rare. (ELS 19)

Indeed, nobody deliberately wants to think except the heroine in a problem play, who frequently gasps out 'I must *think*,' a view fully endorsed by the spectators. 'Let me *think!*' she says; indeed she probably has to go away, to the Riviera, 'to think.' When she comes back we learn that she is now looking for some way to 'stop thinking' – to prevent her from going mad. (HTW 3)

Few men think for themselves. The thoughts of most of us are little more than imitations and adaptations of the ideas of stronger minds. The influence of environment conditions, if it does not control, the mind of man. So it comes about that every age or generation has its dominant and uppermost thoughts, its peculiar way of looking at things and its peculiar basis of opinion on which its col-

lective action and its social regulations rest. All this is largely uncon-
scious. The average citizen of three generations ago was probably
not aware that he was an extreme individualist. The average citizen
of to-day is not conscious of the fact that has ceased to be one. (UR
34–5)

The sad truth is that as yet most of us do not know how to think.
We think we think, but we don't. (GF 49)

TRAVEL

As a further precaution against accident, sleep with the feet towards the [train] engine if you prefer to have the feet crushed, or with the head towards the engine, if you think it best to have the head crushed. In making this decision try to be as unselfish as possible. If indifferent, sleep crosswise with the head hanging over into the aisle. (LL 71)

The battle pictures and the Hall of Mirrors, and the fountains and so on, are, I say, the things best worth seeing at Versailles. Everybody says so. I really wish now that I had seen them. But I am free to confess that I am a poor sightseer at the best. As soon as I get actually in reach of a thing it somehow dwindles in importance. I had a friend once, now a distinguished judge in the United States, who suffered much in this way. He travelled a thousand miles to reach the World's Fair, but as soon as he had arrived at a comfortable hotel in Chicago, he was unable to find the energy to go out to the Fair grounds. He went once to visit Niagara Falls, but failed to see the actual water, partly because it no longer seemed necessary, partly because his room in the hotel looked the other way.

Personally I plead guilty to something of the same spirit. Just where you alight from the steam tramway at Versailles, you will find, close on your right, a little open-air café, with tables under a trellis of green vines. It is as cool a retreat of mingled sun and shadow as I know. There is red wine at two francs and long imported cigars of as soft a flavour as even Louis XIV could have desired. The idea of leaving a grotto like that to go traipsing all over a hot stuffy palace, with a lot of fool tourists, seemed ridiculous. But I bought there a little illustrated book called the *Château de Versailles*, which interested me so extremely that I decided that, on some reasonable opportunity I would go and visit the place. (BB 93–4)

The planet Mars is of special interest inasmuch as its surface shows traces of what are evidently canals which come together at junction points where there must be hotels. It has been frequently proposed [ca. 1926] to interest enough capital to signal to Mars, and it is ingeniously suggested that the signals be *sent in six languages.* (WW 12)

TRUTH

A half-truth, like half a brick, is always more forcible as an argument than a whole one. It carries further. (GF x)

The half-truth is to me a kind of mellow moonlight in which I love to dwell. One sees better in it. (ELS 189)

From the time of the Romans onward Art had of necessity proceeded by the method of selected particulars and conspicuous qualities: that this was the nature and meaning of art itself: that exaggeration (meaning the heightening of the colour to be conveyed) was the very life of it: that herein lay the difference between the photograph ... and the portrait: that by this means and by this means alone could the real truth, – the reality greater than life be conveyed. (ELS 229)

Much that has been written to the disparagement of Charles II is in reality to be ascribed to the essential superiority of his mind. He possessed in an eminent degree that largeness of view, that breadth of mental vision which sees things in their true perspective. He had grasped as but few men have done the great truth that nothing really matters very much. He was able to see that the burning questions of to-day become the forgotten trifles of yesterday, and that the eager controversy of the present fades into the litter of the past. To few it has been given to see things are they are, to know that no opinion is altogether right, no purpose altogether laudable, and no calamity altogether deplorable. To carry in one's mind an abiding sense of the futility of human endeavour and the absurdity of human desire is a sure protection against the malignant narrowness that marks the men endowed with fixed convictions and positive ideas. (ELS 274–5)

∽

In retrospect all our little activities are but as nothing, all that we do has in it a touch of the pathetic, and even our sins and wickedness and crime are easily pardoned in the realization of their futility. (HTT 134)

∽

In thirty-five years of college and public lecturing I always refused to discuss details. It's too late to start now. Let the idea stand for itself. (MDW 206)

∽

Is the world a good place or a bad? An accident or a purpose? Down through the ages in all our literatures echoes the cry of denunciation against the world. *Sunt lachrymae rerum*, mourned the Roman poet – the world is full of weeping; and Shakespeare added, 'All our yesterdays have lighted fools the way to dusty death.' Yet the greatest denunciation is not in the voice of those who cry most loudly. Strutting Hamlet in his velvet suit calls out, 'The time is out of joint,' and egotism echoes it on. But far more poignant is the impotent despair of those whose life has wearied to its end, disillusioned, and who die turning their faces to the wall, still silent.

Is that the whole truth of it? Can life really be like that? With no Santa Claus in it, no element of mystery and wonder, no righteousness to it? It can't be. I remember a perplexed curate of the Church of England telling me that he felt that 'after all, there must be a kind of something.' That's just exactly how I feel about it. There must be something to believe in, life must have its Santa Claus. (RU 118)

For I cannot let Christmas go. Christmas has always seemed to me a day of enchantment, and the world about us on Christmas day, for one brief hour an enchanted world. On Christmas morning the streets are always bright with snow, not too much of it nor too little, hard-frozen snow, all crystals and glittering in the flood of sunshine that goes with Christmas day. ... If there was ever any other Christmas weather I have forgotten it. ... Only the memory of the good remains. ... This enchanted Christmas always seems to me to be a part of that super-self, that higher self that is in each of us, but that only comes to the surface in moments of trial or exaltation and in the hour of death. (RU 121, all but final ellipsis in original)

Seen in this light [of war], how petty are the things we used to fuss and quarrel about, how trivial the make-believe animosities that kept people enemies. I have known two professors of Greek who ceased speaking to one another because of divergent views on the pluperfect subjunctive. I've seen lifelong friends drift apart over golf, just because one could play better but the other counted better. (LaL 88)

Because Pupkin was a brave man now and he knew it and acquired with it all the brave man's modesty. In fact, I believe he was heard to say that he had only done his duty, and that what he did was what any other man would have done: though when somebody else said: 'That's so, when you come to think of it,' Pupkin turned on him that quiet look of the wounded hero, bitterer than words. (SS 113)

For you see, it is the illusion that is the real reality. I think that there are only two people who see clearly (at least as to one another), and these are two young lovers, newly fallen in love. They see one another just as they really are, namely, a Knight Errant and a Fairy. But who realizes that that old feller shuffling along in spats is a Knight Errant, too, and that other is a Fairy, that bent old woman knitting in the corner.

This illusion, greater than reality, we grasp easily in the form of what we call art – our books, our plays. We like to read of people in books, better than ourselves. How quickly we respond to them! So, too, with the drama: 'All the world's a stage,' as Shakespeare said, or at least it could be if we set ourselves to make it so, with each of us idealized into the form of what is really his true self. Come, let us make it so. Let us distribute the parts. Let me see – I'll be the cheery, generous philanthropist – or no, you take that – I'll be the still more cheery fellow, little more than an acquaintance, that he gives the money too. You see, you've heard that I'm hard up (though of course I'm so bright and cheery you'd never guess it) and so you press money on me, or perhaps better, you send me money anonymously; you can start and rehearse it that way at any rate. (LaL 89–90)

People who have never married have not really lived. People who have married and had no children have only half-lived. People who have one child only are a long way from the crown of human life. Old age with nothing to look back upon, nothing to lean upon, is poor stuff as compared with the old age that renews its youth and life and interests in its children and grandchildren. Ask a few lonely old people going out with the tide. (LaL 102)

'This poor old world works hard and gets no richer; thinks hard and gets no wiser; worries much and gets no happier. It casts off old

errors to take on new ones; laughs off ancient superstitions and shiv-
ers over modern ones. It is at best but a Garden of Folly, whose chat-
tering gardeners move a moment among the flowers, waiting for the
sunset.' (GF mock-epigraph, from 'Confucius – or Tutankhamen – I forget
which')

THE WELL-TO-DO

I mix a good deal with the millionaires. I like them. I like their faces.
I like the way they live. I like the things they eat. The more we mix
together the better I like the things we mix. (LL 17)

The creed that was embodied in the words *noblesse oblige* has vanished with the nobility. (DSP 15)

St. Paul's puzzling admonition that every man should pursue every
other man's wealth took on a new meaning. (HL 11)

There are broad steps leading up to the club, so broad and so agree-
ably covered with matting that the physical exertion of lifting oneself from one's motor to the door of the club is reduced to the
smallest compass. The richer members are not ashamed to take the
steps one at a time, first one foot and then the other; and at tight
money periods, when there is a black cloud hanging over the Stock
Exchange, you may see each and every one of the members of the
Mausoleum Club dragging himself up the steps after this fashion,
his restless eyes filled with the dumb pathos of a man wondering
where he can put his hand on half a million dollars. (AA 2)

Now it so happened that there had come a singularly slack moment in the social life of the City. The Grand Opera had sung itself into a huge deficit and closed. There remained nothing of it except the efforts of a committee of ladies to raise enough money to enable Signor Puffi to leave town, and the generous attempt of another committee to gather funds in order to keep Signor Pasti in the City. Beyond this, the opera was dead, though the fact that the deficit was nearly twice as large as it had been the year before showed that public interest in music was increasing. It was indeed a singularly trying time of the year. It was too early to go to Europe, and too late to go to Bermuda. It was too warm to go south, and yet still too cold to go north. In fact, one was almost compelled to stay at home – which was dreadful. (AA 62)

'My dear Dulphie,' whispered Miss Philippa Furlong, the rector's sister (who was at that moment Dulphemia's second self), as they sat behind the new chauffeur, 'don't tell me that he is a chauffeur, because he *isn't*. He can chauffe, of course, but that's nothing.' (AA 64)

I have seen Spugg put aside his glass of champagne – or his glass after he had drunk his champagne – with an expression of something like contempt. He says that he remembers a running creek at the back of his father's farm where he used to lie at full length upon the grass and drink his fill. Champagne, he says, never tasted like that. I have suggested that he should lie on his stomach on the floor of the club and drink a saucerful of soda water. But he won't. (FF 152)

In the course of each summer it is my privilege to do some visiting in the class of the super-rich. By this I mean the class of people who have huge estates at such fashionable places as Nagahucket, and Dogblastit, and up near Lake Owatawetness, where the country is so beautifully wild that it costs a thousand dollars an acre. (WW 70)

Money, big money, is not made from the rich; it is made from the poor. Pennies and cents make plutocrats. (MDW 203)

Hence you can't qualify for being a gentleman by being good, or being honest, or being religious. A gentleman may be those things, but if he is, he never talks about them. In fact a gentleman never speaks of himself and never preaches. All good people do; and so they are not gentlemen. See how perplexing it gets? No wonder it worried us at school. For example can a clergyman be a gentleman? Certainly, if he keeps off religion. Or, for example, would a gentleman steal? He would and he wouldn't. If you left a handful of money right on a table near him, with no one in sight, no one to find out, he wouldn't steal it. Of course not; it's not the kind of thing a gentleman does. But if you left it in a bank account, he might have a go at it; but, of course, that's not exactly stealing; that's embezzlement. Gentlemen embezzle but don't steal. (RU 27).

When we say that this man 'talked like a gentleman,' how then does a gentleman talk? It is not so much a matter of how he talks but how he doesn't talk. No gentleman cares to talk about himself; no gentleman talks about money, or about his family, or about his illness, about the inside of his body or about his soul. Does a gentleman swear? Oh, certainly; but remember, no gentleman would ever swear at a servant – only at his own friends. In point of language a gentleman is not called upon to have any particular choice of words. But he must, absolutely must, have a trained avoidance of them. Any one who says 'them there,' and 'which is yourn' and 'them ain't his'n,' is not a gentleman. There are no two ways about it; he may be 'nature's gentleman'; but that's as far as you can get. (RU 28–9)

In the past, perhaps it was hard to survive without a class system, and to maintain culture, art and science, except at the price of supporting a privileged few. Even at that one looks back, appalled at the 'class' of Victorian England, the easy assumption of merit, the easy tolerance of other people's misery, and the magic lantern of established religion with its peep show for the poor, offering the next world as a substitute for this. (LaL 97–8)

Hitherto unemployment only affected the poor. Now the accursed thing affects the rich. An unforeseen consequence of corporate organization is that the rich may at any time lose their money, without effort or fault of their own. This, in the old days of landed proprietorship, was not possible. Fortunes could not be lost without fault or folly: it needed at least a pack of cards. Hence by a queer twist of human destiny the very rich and the very poor are in the same boat. Such a situation is intolerable. This means economic salvation, or at least salvage, for both. (DP 267)

WOMEN

There are no new girls, no new women. Your grandmother was a devil of a clip half a century before you were born. You telemark on skis; she cut ice in a cutter. You only knew her when she was wrinkled and hobbling, reading the Epistle to the Thessalonians in a lace cap and saying she didn't know what the world was coming to. The young have always been young, and the old always old ... men and women don't change. It took thousands, uncounted thousands, of years to make them what they are. The changes that you think you see lie just on the surface. You could wash them away with soap and hot water. (LaL 7)

She was the most beautiful woman in England. She strode imperiously into the room. She seized a chair imperiously and seated herself on it, imperial side up. (NN 21)

Willowy and slender in form, she was as graceful as a meridian of longitude. Her body seemed almost too frail for motion, while her features were of a mould so delicate as to preclude all thought of intellectual operation. (NN 42–3)

A beautiful creature entered. She evidently belonged to the premises, for she wore no hat and there were white cuffs upon her wrists. She had that indescribable beauty of effectiveness such as is given to hospital nurses. (BB 111)

⚮

I have seen such young witches myself – if I may keep the word: I like it – in colleges such as Wellesley in Massachusetts and Bryn Mawr in Pennsylvania, where there isn't a man allowed within the three-mile limit. To my mind, they do infinitely better thus by themselves. They are freer, less restrained. They discuss things openly in their classes; they lift up their voices, and they speak, whereas a girl in such a place as McGill [ca. 1922], with men all about her, sits for four years as silent as a frog full of shot. (MDE 90)

⚮

I am sure that everybody knows that rather perplexing use of the word 'man.' You've often heard a woman say that for such and such a thing round the house that her husband couldn't do, she had to get a 'man.' Every married woman knows that a husband just goes so far. After that you have to get a 'man.' (RU 84)

⚮

One reason why some men don't care for the society of witty women is because of their own egotism. They want to be *it*. A wise woman sitting down to talk beside such a man will not try to be witty. She will say, 'I suppose you're just as busy as ever!'

All men, you see, have the idea that they are always busy, and if they are not, a woman can soon persuade them that they are. Just say, 'I don't see how you do it all,' without saying what all is. (LaL 4)

⚮

Women should have a *right*, and no doubt will have after the war [WWII], the right to enter any profession. They will even, let us say, enter the church. To many of us it would seem very strange, even repellent, to 'sit under' a woman clergyman preaching from a pulpit.

But this is only prejudice, from our upbringing, not reason; and in any case those of us who think this way don't as a rule go to church. So we won't be there. Indeed, it will give us a new reason for staying away. (LaL 93)

A married woman with children must draw a government salary for being a married woman with children, just as at present an old maid, an *old* one, without children, draws a salary for being an old maid without children. (LaL 100)

Women are, so it often seems to me, our best and at the same time our worst angels. I am not aware that the thought has ever been expressed before, but I say it now, anyway. To my mind a good woman is one of the greatest things on earth, second only perhaps to a good child or a good man. But it is an old, old adage that for a young man at the susceptible age of life, women, and wine and song – are dangerous things. (DP 114)

WORK

Let me sing to you the Nothingness, the Vanity of Life,
Let me teach you of the effort you should shirk,
Let me show you that you never ought to make the least endeavour,
Or indulge yourself in any kind of work. (CoD 125)

Work is when you go in somewhere at seven or eight o'clock in the morning and the boss says 'do this,' and you do it until noon. He says 'I want so and so' and you mustn't say 'Do you?' I have worked once or twice. It's awful. The Indians were quite right about it: it's beneath a human being. (MDW 205)

It is to be noted that the willingness to submit to 'work,' in the true sense, is an acquired capacity which the human race has taken on, with vast advantage to the mass, within the last ten thousand years or so. Some of us have not got it yet. The Portuguese East Africans have not caught on to it. Our Red Indians would have blushed at it, and even in the higher communities, a certain number of individuals – 'tramps,' 'hoboes,' 'loafers' – still don't see it. But the rest of us, along with the horse, the ox, the jackass and the elephant are long since broken into 'work,' to the idea of submitting to the imposition of labour by the hour, often very meaningless in itself, as a condition of living, a sort of compromise between freedom and slavery. (HTW 7–8)

New and feverish desires for luxuries replace each older want as satisfied. The nerves of our industrial civilization are worn thin with the rattle of its own machinery. The industrial world is restless, overstrained and quarrelsome. It seethes with furious discontent, and looks about it eagerly for a fight. It needs a rest. It should be sent, as nerve patients are, to the seaside or the quiet of the hills. Failing this, it should at least slacken the pace of its work and shorten its working day. (UR 146)

If we could in imagination disregard for a moment all question of how the hours of work are to be shortened and how production is to be maintained and ask only what would be the ideal number of the daily hours of compulsory work, for character's sake, few of us would put them at more than four or five. Many of us, as applied to ourselves, at least, would take a chance on character at two. (UR 148–9)

[Men] can hire themselves out and work. Better still, by the industrious process of intrigue rightly called 'busyness,' or business, they may presently get hold of enough of other people's things to live without working. Or again, men can, with a fair prospect of success, enter the criminal class, either in its lower ranks as a house breaker, or in its upper ranks, through politics. (ELS 142)

Labour sees in the immigrant a man who has come to steal his job at lower wages. Foreshorten the picture sufficiently and that is what you see. How would we like it ourselves? How would our college professors like the import of Hindu teachers who could live on nuts and need only a loin-cloth? How would our bankers and financiers appreciate the import of *real* cannibals from the Marquesas? (MDW 184)

[from a letter to a plumber]

I do not wish in any way to seem to reflect upon the apparent dilatoriness with which your work has been done. I am certain that is only apparent and not real. I pass over the fact that my house has now for two weeks been without an adequate water-supply. I do not resent it that you have spent each morning for a fortnight in my kitchen. I am not insensible, sir, to the charm of your presence there under the sink and I recognize the stimulus which it affords to the intellectual life of my cook. I am quite aware, sir, that all of these things are outside of the legitimate scope of complaint. For I understand that they are imposed upon you by your order. It is the command, I believe, of your local union that you must not use a wrench without sending for an assistant: it is an order of your federated brotherhood that you must not handle a screwdriver except in the presence of a carpenter and before witnesses: and it is the positive command of the international order to which you belong that you must not finish any job until it has been declared finishable by a majority vote of the qualified plumbers of your district. These things, no doubt, make for the gayety and variety of industry but interpose, I fear, a check upon the rapidity of your operations. (GF 262-3)

But as to this retirement business, let me give a word of advice to all of you young fellows round fifty. Some of you have been talking of it and even looking forward to it. Have nothing to do with it. Listen; it's like this. Have you ever been out for a late autumn walk in the closing part of the afternoon, and suddenly looked up to realize that the leaves have practically all gone? You hadn't realized it. And you notice that the sun has set already, the day gone before you knew it – and with that a cold wind blows across the landscape. That's retirement. (TMC 175)

WRITING

Writing is thinking. (HTW 1)

※

In a certain sense all literature begins with imitation. Divergence comes later. (HTW 25)

※

You just jot down ideas as they occur to you. The jotting is simplicity itself – it is the occurring which is difficult. (Attributed)

※

I claim that anybody can learn to write, just as anybody can learn to swim. Nor can anybody swim without learning how. A person can thus learn to swim up to the limits imposed by his aptitude and physique. The final result may not be worth looking at, but he can swim. So with writing. (HTW 15)

※

You must write first and 'avoid' afterwards. A writer is in no danger of splitting an infinitive if he has no infinitive to split. (HTW 19)

※

Nor will any amount of disturbance of the ordinary rules of grammar, the freedom called 'poetic license,' in and of itself make poetry, any more than a liquor license can make liquor. (HTW 173)

∾

I did not personally get started writing except for a few odd pieces, until I was forty years old. Like the milkmaid with a fortune in her face I had a fortune (at least as good as hers) in my head ... I had a little initial success with odd humorous writings in the early nineties. I can see now [ca. 1942] that the proportion of success I had was exceptionally high and that the rejection of a manuscript should have meant no more than the blow of a feather. Still more did I fail in not knowing where to find material for literary work. It seemed to me that my life as a resident schoolmaster was so limited and uninteresting that there was nothing in it to write about. Later on, when I had learned how, I was able to turn back to it and write it up with great pecuniary satisfaction. But that was after I had learned how to let nothing get past me. I can write up anything now at a hundred yards. (HTW v–vi)

∾

My obligations to other authorities, in writing this volume, are too many and too various to permit of enumeration. But I may at least express my thanks to myself for the use of four pages out of a book I wrote on the Empire ten years ago. It was an admirable work but, I fear, only read by the proofreader and, even by him, very hurriedly. I express a similar obligation to myself for permission to reproduce in the last chapter the substance of three or four pages of a recent pamphlet. (BE v–vi)

∾

The Victorian Age represents an epoch in the history of letters greater than any that preceded it; greater, in pure letters, it may well be than any about to follow it. (HTT 16)

∾

Life in odd places may be peculiar but I can do without it. I've read enough. If there are any other kind of farmers, share-croppers, hill-

billies, mine workers and such, I'll do without them. I don't care
how hard they swear. (HTW 87)

⊘

It is not possible to separate realistic writing completely from
romantic. The very facts that the writer selects imply a preference
over other facts. (HTW 103)

⊘

A realist is becoming the new name for the man who used to be
called an 'unprincipled scoundrel.' (HTW 104)

⊘

After all, heroism will out, tears will flow. ... The stock in trade of
the romanticist is part of human nature itself. (HTW 103)

⊘

Perhaps we can create a dream world of the past if we cannot make a
real one ... make something which is better than reality ... since
actual life is poor stuff anyway. (HTW 158, ellipses in original)

⊘

The impossible heroines [of nineteenth-century fiction] had to
combine an ideal beauty, an impeccable virtue, a modesty and an
innocence that ran idiocy hard. ... To all her other graces the heroine
added a power of language rarely found outside a legislative assem-
bly. (HTW 105)

⊘

When a detective story gets well started – when the 'body' has been
duly found – and the 'butler' or the 'janitor' have been arrested –
when the police have been completely 'baffled' – then is the time
when the Great Detective is brought in and gets to work.

But before he can work at all, or at least be made thoroughly satisfactory to the up-to-date reader, it is necessary to touch him up. He can be made extremely tall and extremely thin, or even 'cadaverous.' Why a cadaverous man can solve a mystery better than a fat man it is hard to say; presumably the thinner a man is, the more acute is his mind. At any rate, the old school of writers preferred to have their detectives lean. This incidentally gave the detective a face 'like a hawk,' the writer not realizing that a hawk is one of the stupidest of animals. A detective with a face like an orang-outang would beat it all to bits.

Indeed, the Great Detective's face becomes even more important than his body. Here there is absolute unanimity. His face has to be 'inscrutable.' Look at it though you will, you can never read it. Contrast it, for example, with the face of Inspector Higginbottom, of the local police force. Here is a face that can look 'surprised,' or 'relieved,' or, with great ease, 'completely baffled.'

But the face of the Great Detective knows of no such changes. No wonder the Poor Nut, as we may call the person who is supposed to narrate the story, is completely mystified. From the face of the great man you can't tell whether the cart in which they are driving jolts him or whether the food at the Inn gave him indigestion. (SC 207)

We wink our amusement, we wave our goodbye, we shrug our shoulders with disapproval and 'beat our breasts' – at least in race memory – over our sorrow. All of this is preserved in poetry and in the rendering of it. All of this is still seen, in close parallel and resembling it, by anthropologists who study the greater apes. A poet on a platform reciting his verses, with suitable growls and making passes in his hair, is behaving like an ape. They would recognize and welcome him on the Congo. (HTW 182–3)

It is, as I have dared to suggest above, especially in Canada that this new nature poetry grows at its rankest. The really fine Canadian poets, both of the generation just gone by and of the generation now writing [ca. 1943], are too well-known and too well-established to fear criticism of their methods. The fact that most of them owe their success to nature-description-poetry does not make any more tolerable the great mass of the description in verse, whether free or worth money, of the Canadian woods, trees, birds, beasts and waterfalls. Our country is rich in its extent. Granting a thousand poets as the maximum that we could raise they have three thousand square miles for each of them to work on. (HTW 201)

It is appalling the number of things *contracted* by great people in recent fiction. Poor Napoleon, it seems, contracted everything from barber's itch and hay fever to water on the brain. He died just in time to escape the consequences. In fact as a last advice to young writers of historical fiction I would say, Don't write about Napoleon. It isn't fair. He's had enough. (HTW 172)

Transitory popularity is not a proof of genius. But permanent popularity is. (CD 307)

Index: There is no Index
... Of course one has to have an Index. Authors themselves would prefer not to have any. Having none would save trouble and compel reviewers to read the whole book instead of just the Index. (RU 182)

THE END

With it [the universe] goes out in extinction all that was thought of as matter, and with that all the framework of time and space that held it, and the conscious life that matched it. All ends with a cancellation of forces and comes to nothing; and our Universe ends thus with one vast, silent unappreciated joke. (HTT 288)

Cicero and the rest talk of the 'serenity' of old age – in fact, a 'serene' old age has been a phrase in all languages! Serene old Men! Have you ever seen one of them in a sudden temper, because he couldn't find his fishing line, or had lost his ever-sharp pencil? Old age is supposed to be quiet, restful, at peace with all the world. Don't believe it! Old men live in a world of horrors. At a sniff, they are sure the kitchen stove has set fire to the house! The world is closing in on them. They feel that they are going to be overwhelmed at any minute by terrible changes – Bolsheviks, labour agitations, Mussolini – anything!

I remember a year or two ago [ca. 1937], one such stopped me in the street, an old man, just old enough to be getting a nice shake on him even when he stood upright; in fact he had himself buttoned up pretty high in his collar and neckerchief. 'These Bolsheviks!' he said. 'These Bolsheviks, they'll overrun the whole world, mark my words; we'll live to see it!' Well, he didn't, anyway; he blew up the next week. (HML 248–9)

⌀

That strikes again the note of the terrors of old men; they're wearing out, they're running down, and so they get the 'death bug' that ticks and ticks beside their consciousness, so that they feel the flight of time as it goes by, carry a scale of hours and days such as younger people can't imagine. It is as if one looks down an avenue, all lined with evergreen trees – a little mist, indeed, at the end, but the end can't be so far away after all.

So the old men are preoccupied. 'Have you ever,' they whisper, 'had any trouble with your esophagus?' The answer to this is 'Never!' Don't humour or encourage them. Let them take it on the esophagus! They seem to know of parts of the body younger people have never heard of. 'The membranous coating of my diaphragm,' bleats the old fellow, 'is pretty well worn out. I've had to cut out all proteins altogether.'

Cutting them out! They start cutting things out like a captain lightening a ship. 'I cut out whiskey,' says the old fellow, 'and I don't feel any worse for it at all.' No, certainly not; you couldn't feel worse if you tried. 'I've cut tobacco right out.' Certainly, you haven't got suction enough left in you to keep a cigar alight. Then they cut out meat, and cut out coffee, and cut out all the things they know of, and then begin to cut out things that are just names. Ask them; just let them start and they'll tell you they cut out all nitrogen and glycerin, and gun-cotton, and tabloids – the things they cut out would supply a Spanish army. (HML 250)

⌀

Nor is this, I think, the mere complaint of an old man – *Laudator temporis acti* – to whom the grass was green and the sky blue fifty years ago. Some things that old men think might be true, even in this age of Youth. (TMC 140–1)

⌀

Presently, however, as war dies, and poverty vanishes, humanity will begin to be aware that a queer sort of uniformity, something like a great stillness, is coming over the world.

This is beginning now [ca. 1932]. The great 'sameness' which is to envelop and stifle mankind has already begun. Universal communication rapidly begets universal similarity. The word 'standardization' has already come uppermost in the industrial world. Standardized machines turn out products of incomparable uniformity. Divergences and differences drop out. They cost too much. Hence, as the age of the great sameness draws on, all men will more and more be found to be more and more alike, and they will wear the same clothes buttoned in the same way, fashioned probably in a rather infantile style. ...

Outside the schools and colleges will be the great mass of what was once the reading and thinking public – rapidly sifting into something like the accumulated grain in a ten-million-bushel elevator. They will still read the newspaper, the *one* newspaper – the best, so why have any others? – the *World Gazette* published from Patagonia to Peking via New York and London. It will contain the personal news of the important people in the world – there will be, say, about six of them; great world sporting events like the Tom Thumb Golf in the Sahara between the Bolsheviks of Moscow and the Y.M.C.A. of Iowa; great world disasters, such as the upsetting of a train in Patagonia (still not completely organized) with the breaking of the conductor's leg; all of this together with one daily poem – the best in the world, beside which the others are not worth laughing at.

The same public will have that day looked at the world moving picture, and in the evening will all read *the* novel, the same novel, and all fall asleep at the same point in it.

Meantime human life, its care gone, its digestion rotating as smoothly as a sleeping gyroscope, lapsed in ease and with preventive medicine at its elbow, will grow longer and longer. From the fifty years it has now reached in its recent sudden advance it will move to seventy, to eighty, to ninety, and still onward. Little old clean-shaven

men will sit down to bridge for the fifty-thousandth time, with part-
ners they knew a hundred years ago.

The lengthened and assured span of life will bring with it a new
dreariness. There will be no death, except by an accident – odd,
exceptional, awful, a thing to be shuddered at – or by the extreme
weariness of old age, a slow and imperceptible sleep, the parting
from a world already long forgotten and unregretted. Human life
will have been lengthened, but not the soul and the freshness of it
that belong only to life's morning. After that, life will stretch in front
of each, in a long vista, visible to an infinite distance of dreariness,
like a trail across a desert.

Thus will the human race sink, generation after generation, into a
slow stagnation that will lead it unconsciously to oblivion. The restless survival instinct, that fought its wars, and chafed at its poverty,
and cared for its young and its own, this will fade out, and with it
the power to live.

Then in some far future there will come the great mortality – not
a pestilence, not a plague – just a great mortality – and the human
race, like lone islanders upon a rock, will perish to the last man.
(DP 268–71)

∽

In short, I should like to be allowed to pass a word of advice to the
astronomers and geologists. Don't announce these things ahead in
this alarming way. Wait till they happen and then feature them up
large when they're worth while.

I understand that there are lots of other geological and astronomical disasters coming. It seems that the coast line of both New
England and England itself is falling into the sea. A whole barrow-
load of dirt that was left near Shoreham by William the Conqueror
has fallen in. Old Winchelsea and St. Michaels have rolled under the
water. Passamaquoddy Bay is engulfing New Brunswick. Never
mind. Let us eat, drink, and be merry. We don't need to board on
Passamaquoddy Bay.

The sun, it seems, is burning out. A few more billion years and its last flicker will fade. Many of the stars are dead already and others dying. The moon is gone – a waste of dead rocks in a glare of reflected light. Even empty space is shrinking and puckering into curves like a withering orange.

Courage! Forget it! Let us go right on like a band of brothers while it lasts. (IM 43–4)

∽

THREE SCORE AND TEN: THE BUSINESS OF GROWING OLD

Old age is the 'Front Line' of life, moving into No Man's Land. No Man's Land is covered with mist. Beyond it is Eternity. As we have moved forward, the tumult that now lies behind us has died down. The sounds grow less and less. It is almost silence. There is an increasing feeling of isolation, of being alone. We seem so far apart. Here and there one falls, silently, and lies a little bundle on the ground that the rolling mist is burying. Can we not keep nearer? It's hard to see one another. Can you hear me? Call to me. I am alone. This must be near the end.

I have been asked how old age feels, how it feels to have passed seventy, and I answer in metaphor, as above, 'not so good.'

Now let us turn it round and try to laugh it off in prose. It can't be so bad as that, eh, what? Didn't Cicero write a book on old age to make it all right? But you say he was only just past sixty when he wrote it, was he? That's a tough one. Well, what about Rabbi ben Ezra, you remember – 'Grow old along with me.' Oh he was eighty-one, eh? No thanks, I'll stay right here around seventy. He can have all his fun for himself at eighty-one.

I was born in Swanmoor, a suburb of Ryde in the Isle of Wight, on December 30, 1869. That was in Victorian England at its most Victorian, far away now, dated by the French Empire, still glittering, and Mr. Dickens writing his latest book on the edge of the grave while I thought out my first on the edge of my cradle and, in America, dated by people driving golden spikes on Pacific railroads.

It was a vast, illimitable world, far superior to this – whole continents unknown, Africa just an outline, oceans never sailed, ships lost over the horizon – as large and open as life itself.

Put beside such a world as this present shrunken earth, its every corner known, its old-time mystery gone with the magic of the sea, to make place for this new demoniac confine, loud with voices out of emptiness and tense with the universal threat of death. This is not mystery but horror. The waves of the magic sea called out in the sunlight: 'There must be a God.' The demoniac radio answers in the dark: 'There can't be.' Belief was so easy then; it has grown so hard now; and life, the individual life, that for an awakening child was so boundless, has it drawn into this – this alley-way between tall cypresses that must join somewhere in the mist? But stop, we are getting near No Man's Land again. Turn back.

Moving pictures love to give us nowadays [ca. 1942] 'cavalcades' of events to mark the flight of time. Each of us carries his own. Mine shows, as its opening, the sea beaches of the Isle of Wight. ... Then turn on Portchester village and its Roman castle. ... Queen Victoria going past in a train, in the dark, putting her head out of the window (her eight heads out of eight windows). ... Now shift to an Atlantic sailing steamer (type of 1876) with people emigrating to Canada. ... Then a Canadian farm in a lost corner of Ontario up near Lake Simcoe for six years. ... Put in bears, though there weren't any ... boarding school, scenes at Upper Canada College – the real old rough stuff ... University, cap and gown days, old style; put a long beard on the president; show fourteen boarding-houses at $4.50 a week. ... School teaching – ten years – (run it fast – I want to forget it). ...

Then make the film Chicago University with its saloons of forty years ago, a raw place, nowhere to smoke. ... And then settle the film down to McGill University, and run it round and round as slowly as you like for thirty-six sessions – college calling in the Autumn, stu-

dents and co-eds and Rah! Rah! all starting afresh, year after year. ...
College in the snow, the February classroom; hush! don't wake them,
it's a lecture in archaeology. ... All of it again and again. ... College
years, one after the other. ... Throw in, as interludes, journeys to
England, a lecture trip around the Empire. ... Put in Colombo, Cey-
lon, for atmosphere. ... Then more college years. ...

Then loud music and the Great War with the college campus all
at drill, the boys of yesterday turned to men. ... Then the war over,
lecture trips to the U.S. ... Pictures of Iowa State University. ...
Ladies' Fortnightly Club – about forty of them. ... Then back to the
McGill campus. ... Retirement. ... An honorary degree ('this venerable scholar'). ... And then unexpectedly the war again and the Black
Watch back on the McGill campus.

Such is my picture, the cavalcade all the way down from the
clouds of the morning to the mists of the evening.

As the cavalcade passes down the years it is odd how gradually and
imperceptibly the change of outlook comes, from the eyes of wonder to those of disillusionment – or is it to those of truth? A child's
world is full of celebrated people, wonderful people like the giants
and magicians of the picture books. Later in life the celebrated people are all gone. There aren't any – or not made of what it once
meant.

I recall from over half a century ago a prize-day speaker at Upper
Canada College telling us that he saw before him the future states-
men, the poets, the generals and the leaders of the nation. I thought
the man a nut to say that. What he saw was just us. Yet he turned
out to be correct; only in a sense he wasn't; it was still only us after
all. It is the atmosphere of illusion that cannot last.

Yet some people, I know, are luckier in this than I am. They're
born in a world of glamour and live in it. For them there are great
people everywhere, and the illusion seems to feed itself. One such I
recall out of the years, with a capacity for admiration all his own.

'I sat next to Professor Buchan at the dinner last night,' he once
told me. 'He certainly is a great scholar, a marvelous philologian!'

'Is he?' I said.

'Yes,' my friend continued. 'I asked him if he thought the Indian word *snabe* was the same as the German word *knabe*.'

'And what did he say?'

'He said he didn't know.'

And with that my friend sat back in quiet appreciation of such accurate scholarship and of the privilege of being near it. There are many people like that, decent fellows to be with. Their illusions keep their life warm.

But for the most of us they fade out, and life itself as we begin to look back on it appears less and less. Has it all faded to this? There comes to me the story of an old Carolina negro who found himself, after years of expectancy, privileged to cast a vote. After putting the ballot paper in the box he stood, still expectant, waiting for what was to happen, to come next. And then, in disillusionment: 'Is that all there is, boss? Is that all there is to it?'

'That's all,' said the presiding officer.

So it is with life. The child says 'when I am a big boy' – but what is that? The boy says 'when I grow up' – and then, grown up, 'when I get married.' But to be married, once done and over, what is that again? The man says 'when I can retire' – and then when retirement comes he looks back over the path traversed, a cold wind sweeps over the fading landscape and he feels somehow that he has missed it all. For the reality of life, we learn too late, is in the living tissue of it from day to day, not in the expectation of better, nor in the fear of worse. Those two things, to be always looking ahead and to worry over things that haven't yet happened and very likely won't happen – those take the very essence out of life.

If one could only live each moment to the full, in a present, intense with its own absorption, even if as transitory and evanescent as Einstein's 'here' and 'now.' It is strange how we cry out in our collective human mind against this restless thinking and clamour for time to stand still – longing for a land where it is always afternoon, or for a book of verses underneath a bough where we may let the world pass.

But perhaps it is this worry, this restlessness, that keeps us on our necessary path of effort and endeavour. Most of us who look back from old age have at least a comfortable feeling that we have 'got away with it.' At least we kept out of jail, out of the asylum and out of the poor house. Yet one still needs to be careful. Even 'grand old men' get fooled sometimes. But at any rate we don't want to start over; no, thank you, it's too hard. When I look back at long evenings of study in boarding-house bedrooms, night after night, one's head sinking at times over the dictionary – I wonder how I did it.

And school days – at Upper Canada College anno Domini 1882 – could I stand that now? If some one asked me to eat 'supper' at six and then go and study next day's lessons, in silence in the long study from seven to nine-thirty – how would that be? A school waiter brought round glasses of water on a tray at half-past eight, and if I asked for a whisky and soda could I have had it? I could not. Yet I admit there was the fun of putting a bent pin – you know how, two turns in it – on the seat where the study master sat. And if I were to try that now at convocation they wouldn't understand it. Youth is youth, and age is age.

So many things, I say, that one went through seem hopelessly difficult now. Yet other things, over which youth boggles and hesitates and palpitates, seem so easy and so simple to old age. Take the case of women, I mean girls. Young men in love go snooping around, hoping, fearing, wondering, lifted up at a word, cast down by an eyebrow. But if he only knew enough, any young man – as old men see it – could have any girl he wanted. All he need do is to step up to her and say, 'Miss Smith, I don't know you, but your overwhelming beauty forces me to speak; can you marry me at, say, three-thirty this afternoon?'

I mean that kind of thing in that province of life would save years of trepidation. It's just as well, though, that they don't know it or away goes all the pretty world of feathers and flounces, of flowers and dances that love throws like a gossamer tissue across the path of life.

On such a world of youth, old age can only gaze with admiration. As people grow old all youth looks beautiful to them. The plainest girls are pretty with nature's charms. The dullest duds are at least young. But age cannot share it. Age must sit alone.

The very respect that young people feel for the old – or at least for the established, the respectable, by reason of those illusions of which I spoke – makes social unity impossible. An old man may think himself a 'hell of a feller' inside, but his outside won't justify it. He must keep to his corner or go 'ga-ga,' despised of youth and age alike. ...

In any case, to put it mildly, old men are tiresome company. They can't listen. I notice this around my club. We founded it thirty years ago and the survivors are all there, thirty years older than they were thirty years ago, and some even more, much more. Can they listen? No, not even to me. And when they start to tell a story they ramble on and on, and you know the story anyway because it's the one you told them yesterday. Young people when they talk have to be snappy and must butt in and out of conversation as they get a chance. But once old men are given rope, you have to pay it out to them like a cable. To my mind the only tolerable old men are the ones – you notice lots of them when you look for them – who have had a stroke – not a tragic one; that would sound cruel – but just one good flap of warning. If I want to tell a story, I look round for one of these.

The path through life I have outlined from youth to age, you may trace for yourself by the varying way in which strangers address you. You begin as 'little man' and 'little boy,' because a little man is littler than a little boy; then 'sonny' and then 'my boy' and after that 'young man' and presently the interlocutor is younger than yourself and says, 'Say, mister.' I can still recall the thrill of pride I felt when a Pullman porter first called me 'doctor' and when another one raised me up to 'judge,' and the terrible shock it was when a taxi man swung open his door and said, 'Step right in, dad.'

It was hard to bear when a newspaper reporter spoke of me as the 'old gentlemen,' and said I was very simply dressed. He was a liar;

those were my best things. It was worse shock when a newspaper first called me a septuagenarian, another cowardly lie, as I was only sixty-nine and seven-twelfths. Presently I shall be introduced as 'this venerable old gentleman' and the axe will fall when they raise me to the degree of 'grand old man.' That means on our continent any one with snow-white hair who has kept out of jail till eighty. That's the last and worst they can do to you.

Yet there is something to be said even here for the mentality of age. Old people grow kinder in their judgment of others. They are able to comprehend, even if not to pardon, the sins and faults of others. If I hear of a man robbing a cash register of the shop where he works, I think I get the idea. He wanted the cash. If I read of a man burning down his store to get the insurance, I see that what he wanted was the insurance. He had nothing against the store. Yet somehow just when I am reflecting on my own kindliness I find myself getting furious with a waiter for forgetting the Worcester sauce.

This is the summary of the matter that as for old age there's nothing to it, for the individual looked at by himself. It can only be reconciled with our view of life insofar as it has something to pass on, the new life of children and grandchildren, or if not that, at least some recollection of good deeds, or of something done that may give one the hope to say, *non omnis moriar* (I shall not altogether die).

Give me my stick. I going out on to No Man's Land. I'll face it. (RU 174–9)